Henry Martin Duffield

The Centennial Celebration of the Evacuation of Detroit by the British

Henry Martin Duffield

The Centennial Celebration of the Evacuation of Detroit by the British

ISBN/EAN: 9783337154943

Printed in Europe, USA, Canada, Australia, Japan

Cover: Foto ©ninafisch / pixelio.de

More available books at **www.hansebooks.com**

On July 11th, 1796, Fort Lernoult at Detroit was
Evacuated by the British, the United States
took possession, and the American Flag
was first raised over Detroit.

VIEW OF DETROIT IN 1796.
From a sketch in possession of C. M. Burton, Esq.

THE

CENTENNIAL CELEBRATION

OF THE

EVACUATION OF DETROIT BY THE BRITISH.

JULY 11, 1796---JULY 11, 1896.

REPORT OF THE PROCEEDINGS, WITH THE ADDRESSES OF
COL. H. M. DUFFIELD, SENATOR J. C. BURROWS,
AND PRESIDENT JAS. B. ANGELL.

DETROIT.
PRINTED FOR THE COMMITTEE.
1896

JOHN F. EBY & COMPANY, PRINTERS.
65-67 CONGRESS WEST.

INTRODUCTORY NOTE.

When the War of Independence began in the east its effects were almost immediately felt in Detroit, and early in 1775 the English made this post the chief military depot in the west, and the fitting-out place for the forays to be made upon the settlements in Kentucky, Virginia and Pennsylvania. The evident intent was to keep the colonists in the west so busy defending their homes that they would be unable to help their brethren in the east.

With this object in view millions of dollars worth of goods were shipped to Detroit and distributed to the Indians who were invited here and came by thousands from the west and south. On their arrival they were feasted and flattered without stint; clothing, trinkets, fire arms, and "red-handled scalping knives" were supplied to them in enormous quantities, and on returning from their forays they often brought hundreds of scalps and prisoners.

The defeat of the English in the west was largely decided by the capture of Gov. Henry Hamilton of Detroit, at Vincennes, by Col. George Rogers Clark, on March 5th, 1779. That victory and American successes in the east, brought about the treaties of 1782 and 1783, which provided for the surrender of the western territory by the English. The pretext of unsettled claims, and the protests of Montreal fur traders, who derived immense revenues from this region, delayed the surrender.

Meanwhile the Indians continued their depredations, but finally, on August 30th, 1794, they and their British allies were effectually defeated by Major General Anthony Wayne, at Fort Miami, and a way was opened for the conclusion of the war.

The final treaty of peace, known as Jay's treaty, was made November 19th, 1794; it provided for the evacuation of Detroit and other western posts on or before June 1st, 1796. Owing, however, to various obstacles the surrender did not take place until July 11th, 1796. On that day at 12 o'clock noon, the English flag was hauled down from the flag staff of Fort Lernoult at Detroit, and the same day the fort was taken possession of by Captain Moses Porter, with a detachment of sixty-five men from General Wayne's army, Colonel John F. Hamtramck arriving two days later.

The surrender of Detroit on July 11th, 1796, clearly marks the date of the actual ownership by the United States of a territory larger than the original thirteeen states, and the final results of such ownership gave us not only the control of the Great Lakes, but the Mississippi as well, and, indeed, of all the territory clear to the Pacific coast.

REV. RUFUS CLARK, D. D.,
Rector of St. Paul's Church, Detroit.

EVENTS WHICH LED UP TO THE CELEBRATION OF THE CENTENNIAL OF EVACUATION DAY.

At the banquet of the Michigan Society of the Sons of the American Revolution, on February 22d, 1896, Rev. Rufus W. Clark offered the following resolutions:

"Whereas, the eleventh day of July will mark the one hundredth anniversary of the evacuation by the British of our territory and the raising of the Stars and Stripes over the City of Detroit, this day is deserving of more than passing mention, none being more important to us, as Americans and as citizens of this municipality. This is a day upon which we may well commemorate the achievements of our fathers, the founders of this republic, and encourage sentiments of love and devotion to our country. It is a day that should be seized upon especially by members of this society, to remind a rising generation of their priceless heritage in a land no longer dominated by a foreign power.

"1. Resolved, That the day shall be observed by the Michigan Society of the Sons of the American Revolution as a time for special rejoicing and for convening the members of this society.

"2. Resolved, As the day belongs not only to us, but to all patriotic citizens, that a committee of five be appointed by the chairman of this meeting to consult with the city officials, the military authorities at Fort Wayne and patriotic societies of Detroit and arrange, if possible, upon a plan for the suitable public celebration of the day, and for such meetings as befit so rare and important an occasion."

The resolutions being adopted, Rev. Mr. Clark moved that Mr. Fred. T. Sibley be made chairman of the committee on celebration. He thought no one more suitable than a grandson of Solomon Sibley, the first mayor of Detroit, and a man stalwart in all that made for the good of Detroit, also a chief justice of the supreme bench, could be found to head the committee. Mr. Thomas Jerome seconded the nomination in a patriotic speech, and ex-Senator Palmer supported the nomination.

The chairman, Col. Henry M. Duffield, named the celebration committee, as follows: Frederick T. Sibley, Rev. Rufus W. Clark, Thomas Jerome, J. C. Smith, Jr., and Oliver H. Phelps.

A conference of the various patriotic societies, proposed by the Society of the Sons of the American Revolution, February 22d, 1896, was held at the parlors of the Russell House, in Detroit, on May 22d.

The first meeting of the General Committee was held at the Loyal Legion rooms May 25th, at which Gen. R. A. Alger presided. There were present: Capt. Cornelius Gardener, U. S. A., Don M. Dickinson, E. B. Welton, James Vernor, Rev. Rufus W. Clark, Silas Farmer, Frank J. Hecker, and Thomas S. Jerome. Mr. Jerome was elected secretary. Rev. R. W. Clark stated the objects of the meeting.

It was moved and carried that a celebration be held on July 11th.

At a subsequent meeting the committee appointed by the chair to name the various committees, reported as follows:

GROUP OF COMMITTEEMEN.

1. JAMES T. STERLING,
2. FRANK J. HECKER,
3. JOHN N. BAGLEY,
4. CHARLES B. HULL,
5. HARRY F. CHIPMAN,
6. REV. RUFUS W. CLARK,
7. ELLIOTT T. SLOCUM,
8. GEN. A. L. BRESLER,
9. SILAS FARMER,
10. THOMAS S. JEROME,
11. DON M. DICKINSON.

R. A. Alger, General Chairman.

Executive Committee.

Henry M. Duffield, Chairman. Thomas S. Jerome, Sec'y.
E. T Slocum. Frank J. Hecker.
Together with the Chairmen of the various Sub-Committees.

Entertainment Committee.

W. H. Elliott, Chairman. A. L. Stephens.
Hervey C. Parke. R. Phelps.
M. S. Smith. R. H. Fyfe.
W. C. Maybury. J. B. Moore.
T. D. Buhl. W. A. Butler, Jr.
D. J. Campau. W. V. Moore.
W. J. Chittenden. M. W. O'Brien.
Collins B. Hubbard.

Programme Committee.

Rufus W. Clark, Chairman. John N. Bagley.
James Vernor. Charles Flowers.
Henry S. Sibley. E. T. Slocum.

Tablet Committee.

Silas Farmer, Chairman. Louis A. Arthur.
A. H. Griffith.

Parade Committee.

James T. Sterling, Chairman. August Goebel.
Cornelius Gardener, U. S. A. Charles Dupont.
H. B. Lothrop. Charles Reid.
John Atkinson. Gilbert Wilkes.
A. L. Bresler.

Press Committee.

James E. Scripps, Chairman. W. Livingstone, Jr.
A. G. Boynton. P. C. Baker.
J. J. Emery.

Music Committee.

John N. Bagley, Chairman.
S. T. Douglas.
F. W. Eddy.
Ford D. C. Hinchman.

Finance Committee.

George H. Russel, Chairman.
George N. Brady.
A. E. F. White.
James E. Davis.
George H. Hopkins.
Charles Dean.
Marvin Preston.
Charles Wright.
Charles Stinchfield.
John T. Shaw.
E. B. Welton.
R. W. Jacklin.
Hamilton Dey.

Invitation Committee.

Don M. Dickinson, Chairman.
Thomas W. Palmer.
Simon Snyder, U. S. A.
Allan Shelden.
William C. McMillan.

Carriage Committee.

Charles B. Hull, Chairman.
George H. Barbour.
S. S. Babcock.
F. T. Moran.
Strathearn Hendrie.

Badge Committee.

Frank H. Walker, Chairman.
W. G. Thompson.
H. M. Campbell.
Clarence Carpenter.
Harry B. Joy.

Committee in Charge of Building.

Harry F. Chipman, Chairman.
E W. Cottrell.
F. E. Farnsworth.
R. G. Butler.
Peter Diederich.
Edwin Henderson.
Arthur L. Holmes.

HON. JOHN T. RICH,
Governor of Michigan.

THE GOVERNOR'S PROCLAMATION.

To the People of the State of Michigan:

For many years after the cessation of active hostilities between Great Britain and the United States in the Revolutionary War, the British refused to carry out the terms of the peace and surrender to the Americans the territory they had won, and it was not until the 11th of July, 1796, at Detroit, that the British flag finally ceased to float over any part of the country whose independence had been acknowledged thirteen years before.

It is proposed to recognize the centennial of the evacuation of Detroit by the British, by a celebration at Detroit on the 11th day of next July. The importance of this event to the nation, and especially to the great middle and western states, demands fitting recognition from the executive of the state, and every citizen who can do so is earnestly urged to attend the celebration of the anniversary of this memorable event.

The definite and final yielding up of this western region gave the Federal government the control not only of the great lakes, but eventually of the Mississippi as well, and indeed, in its finality, of all our western territory clear to the Pacific coast.

On that date the American flag with its fifteen stars was first raised over our soil, and its raising meant the speedy founding of the states of Michigan, Ohio, Indiana, Illinois, Wisconsin and Minnesota.

With the raising of the flag on July 11, 1796, British domination over any part of our country ceased, the "rebels" then living here breathed freely, and the way was opened for all the blessings we now enjoy as a part of the United States of America.

In historic interest and importance no other date in connection with the west is of equal value, for the surrender of Detroit marked the close of the War of the Revolution and the final accomplishment of the results fought for by our fathers during so many years, and the date of that event should excite patriotic loyalty in the breast of every member of the commonwealth and be treasured in the memory of every citizen.

Given under my hand and the great seal of the State, at the capitol, in Lansing, this 24th day of June, in the year of our Lord one thousand eight hundred and ninety-six, and of the independence of the United States the one hundred and twentieth.

JOHN T. RICH.

By the Governor,
    WASHINGTON GARDNER,
        Secretary of State.

THE CELEBRATION.

Saturday, the 11th of July, 1896, was a bright, clear and beautiful day, rather warm, but not excessively so. The patriotism of Detroit was fully aroused, and the city was gay with flags and streamers of the national colors. The City Hall had been decorated at a cost of over $500 alone. A great many people had come into the city from the interior of the State, and the streets were thronged throughout the day.

Appropriately, the public exercises were held in the unfinished Federal Building, which occupies the exact site of Fort Lernoult, surrendered to the United States on July 11th, 1796. The interior had been fitted up for the occasion, under the superintendence of Harry F. Chipman, chairman of the committeee on building. On the north side a spacious platform had been erected, capable of accommodating some 700 persons. In front of the platform, the unfinished brick floor, covered with sawdust, was seated with about 3,000 chairs. A railed-in passage way extended from the platform steps to the Fort street entrance. To the west of this, admission was had by tickets distributed by the members of the various committees; to the east, entrance from Shelby street, tickets were not required. It was estimated that 3,500 persons were present during the exercises.

The decorations of the building were very effective. From the open girders overhead depended festoons of red, white and blue bunting, through which the sun's rays produced a most beautiful effect. Over the speakers' stand hung the American flag and a large portrait of George Washington. The rough brick walls were decorated with the flags and arms of the several states comprised in the old northwestern territory, possession of which was secured by the United States by the evacuation of Detroit, the event celebrated. The iron columns were covered with colored cloth and gaily decorated. At the left of the speakers' stand stood a section of the flag staff of the old fort, recovered some years ago in making an excavation on the site, and now in possession of the Detroit Museum of Art.

On the platform were seated the following organizations:

The Officers of the City Government.
The Sons of the American Revolution.
The Daughters of the American Revolution.
The Daughters of the War of 1812.
The Michigan Society of Colonial Dames of America.
The Loyal Legion.
Fairbanks Post, Grand Army of the Republic.
Detroit Post, Grand Army of the Republic.
John Brown Post, Grand Army of the Republic.
Girls' Auxiliary of Farquhar Post No. 162.
Women's Relief Corps.
U. S. Grant Command, Union Veterans' Union.
Mexican Veterans, including Col. H. S. Dean, Geo. W. Walters, S. W. Perry and Oliver Geary.

Among other occupants of the platform were: His Excellency Gov. John T. Rich, accompanied by his staff—Gen. W. S. Green, Gen. J. H. Kidd, Gen. Joseph Walsh, Col. W. A. Gavett, Col. Lou Burt, Lieut.-Col. W. W. Cook and Lieut.-Col. S. H. Avery, all in full uniform; Gen. R. A. Alger, Col. Henry M. Duffield, Hon. J. C. Burrows, President James B. Angell of the University of Michigan; Rt. Rev. G. Mott Williams, D. D., Bishop of Marquette; Charles Flowers, City Counsellor; Rt. Rev. John S. Foley, D. D., Roman Catholic Bishop of Detroit; Hon. Henry M. Swan, U. S. District Judge; Hon. Claudius B. Grant, Hon. J. B. Moore and Hon. Frank A. Hooker, Justices of the Supreme Court of Michigan; Judge Wm. L. Carpenter and Judge George S. Hosmer of the Wayne Circuit Court; State Treasurer J. M. Wilkinson; Prof. A. C. McLaughlin of the State University; ex-Congressman Wm. C. Maybury; Joseph T. Jacobs, of Ann Arbor, member of the U. S. Indian Commission; Capt. Hinds, of Stanton; J. Q. A. Sessions, of Ann Arbor; Col. J. S. Farrar, of Mt. Clemens; George Newell, of Flint; Robert Campbell, of Ann Arbor; Gen. Luther S. Trowbridge, Maj. James Vincent, Dexter M. Ferry, Col. Frank J. Hecker, the members of the executive committee, and W. R. Shelby, of Grand Rapids, a great-grandson of Gov. Shelby of Kentucky after whom Fort Shelby was named. Mr. Shelby had with him a spyglass captured from one of the British ships at the battle of Lake Erie by Commodore Perry.

While waiting for the audience to arrive and become seated, the Metropolitan Band played a number of patriotic airs.

THE PUBLIC EXERCISES.

At 10:30 o'clock the chairman of the day, Gen. R. A. Alger, called the great assemblage to order and read the following opening address:

Fellow Citizens—We gather upon this historic spot to-day to commemorate the last act of our heroic forefathers in the War of the Revolution.

It was upon these grounds, occupied by this stately building, that old Fort Lernoult was situated; a fort erected by the British army to resist the assaults of those patriots who were battling for the liberty they won—the liberty we enjoy to-day.

It was here, one hundred years ago to-day, that the flag of the enemy was hauled down, and our own Stars and Stripes run to the mast head, then with but fifteen stars in its azure field—to-day, forty-five; the flag that was never lowered to any foe, and floats over the richest and best nation in the world.

In no boastful spirit do we come, nor in vain-glorious triumph at our victory, but with a just pride in the valor of our ancestors, and thankfulness to Almighty Providence that the ground broken by the sword of war has borne to us the blessed fruits of peace.

The history of the world is marked by epochs of war, and the chief glory of every nation is the valor of its defenders. It is well that this is so, for in our peaceful pursuits, we are too apt to forget the cost of the blessings we enjoy, and not until the drum sounds the signal to arms, is it that we stop to consider what it costs to build or save a nation.

GEN. R. A. ALGER.
Ex-Governor of Michigan.

As in the frequent experience of individuals, the bitterest enemies, reconciled, form the strongest ties of friendship, so with nations—those which do battle with each other, when peace is declared, often make the strongest allies.

As we are at peace with the mother country to-day and look upon its people with no envy as they live under the benign rule of their mother queen, so may we hope that war shall never again come between us. We are too great to boast, too strong to fear invasion. We covet the possessions of no other nation, nor do we fear for the safety of our own. To us all to-day war is but an echoing memory, and not an expectation.

Among us here to-day are veterans of the Mexican War, and many of that grand host whose courage crushed the standards of secession and wove the web of our destiny into eternal unity.

To them and those of their comrades who returned not with them, to enjoy the fruits of their sacrifice, I know a grateful people will ever rise up to give the meed of praise they so fairly won.

Detroit welcomes here to-day, many distinguished guests. It presents no battlements or ramparts to the view, as it needs none for its protection, but in their stead shows you busy factories, whose belching mouths, night and day, blacken the sky with the smoke of industry. These are the truest monuments to the peace whose noble path was cut by war.

Rt. Rev. G. Mott Williams, D. D., then offered prayer, as follows:

THE PRAYER.

O God of our fathers, our hope and strength, we bless thy Holy Name for the faith of those great men who won our independence and framed the constitutional government of these United States. We bless thee for the inheritance of civil and religious liberty, and for the many shining examples of patriotism given us by citizens of this land in peace and war.

We thank thee that so many of those who have been welcomed to our shores, while needing an asylum, have rendered the State so good an account for her charity, and we pray thee that the first acquisition of those who come to us may be a love of their fostering mother.

We thank thee for boundaries so vast, so inclusive, so rich and so commanding, for the great gift of national independence, and because thy wise providence in severing the ties which bound us to the motherland, left us still in laws, character and customs the best part of the inheritance of the Anglo-Saxon race.

We bless thee that the transfer of government which we celebrate to-day was made in peace and not in war, a result of treaties, not of blows, of reason, not of force, and we especially thank thee that this peaceful transfer of government between kindred peoples has been followed by so many years of honorable peace, but once broken, and now for four-score years unmarred.

And we beseech thee that the present peace of this frontier may continue by thy favor, and by the virtue, the self-control, the wisdom and brotherliness of these peoples, and that we especially may walk worthy of high calling among the nations.

THE TABLET.

We confess, O God, our manifold shortcomings as men, as citizens and as a nation; forgive us, but forsake us not.

Let there be peace and truth in our days, pure religion and domestic happiness. Bless the President and every arm of government; sanctify our lives, our families, our homes and our schools; make us love our country truly and honestly; and grant the course of the whole world may be so peacefully ordered by thy government that thy church may joyfully serve thee in all godly quietness through Jesus Christ, our Lord, according to whose teaching we are bold to say:

Our Father, who art in Heaven, hallowed be thy name, etc. Amen!

The Boylston Club then led in the singing of the hymn, "My Country, 'tis of Thee," in which the entire audience heartily joined.

UNVEILING OF THE MEMORIAL TABLET.

While the band played the "Star Spangled Banner," the chairman, together with Mr. Shelby, representing the Sons of the American Revolution, and Mr. Silas Farmer, representing the committee, proceeded to the Fort street entrance, where the tablet has been placed by a special Act of Congress. The invited guests, and the presidents and commanders of the patriotic societies were also there assembled.

In their presence and before the throng outside of the building, Gen. Alger withdrew the veiling and said: "In behalf of the heroes who gave us this land of liberty, and in remembrance of them, I humbly unveil this tablet."

The flag was then raised upon the Federal Building and a salute of twenty-one guns was then fired by the United States Revenue Cutter "Fessenden," at anchor in the Detroit River.

When all had returned to the platform the chairman said that it had been expected that Mayor Hazen S. Pingree would be present to welcome the distinguished guests, but in his absence, Hon. Charles Flowers, City Counselor, would perform that duty.

THE ADDRESS OF WELCOME.
BY HON. CHARLES FLOWERS.

The City of Detroit, upon this centennial day, gives greeting and welcome to the men and women whose forefathers, by reason of their sublime courage, and their fidelity to a living and glowing principle, made it necessary for their foes to strike their flag, and bid farewell to so fair and so vast an empire.

To the descendants of the brave men who lingered upon the shores of this majestic river, the City of Detroit also gives greeting and welcome. With them we have no quarrel. The hour struck in the fateful history of the world for those of one language, one religion and one blood, to stand upon the broad road of national life, where the ways parted. The day of separation had come.

It is well for us to remember those days. The patriotic heart has not grown cold. The genius of greed has not wholly possessed the land. Amid the sound and fury and madness of partisan strife, amid the insane thirst and hunger for power and advantage, the attentive ear can still catch, as coming from a million breasts, the breathings of a spirit, responsive to the agony of those who suffered with Washington at Valley Forge, responsive to the ecstasy of those who rejoiced with him at Yorktown.

The City of Detroit gives greeting and welcome to you all. It does not ask your nationality or your faith. It only asks if you are true to the cause of individual liberty and equality, the principles represented by the beautiful banner, which upon this golden day so peacefully and so solemnly floats above your heads.

Messrs. Homer Warren and Robert Murray then sang "The Sword of Bunker Hill." They alternated in singing the verses, and both were cheered most heartily, and were compelled to repeat the last verse.

Gen. Alger said he would introduce a brave soldier well known throughout the state to make the historical address, and Col. Duffield was loudly applauded as he came to the speaking stand. He was listened to with close and noiseless attention. His address was as follows:

THE HISTORICAL ADDRESS.
BY COL. HENRY M. DUFFIELD.

The scene of the last act in the great drama of the Revolutionary War—its final triumph—was laid in Detroit. One hundred years ago the British troops evacuated this post and with them departed the last vestige of England's rule from the northwest.

To understand its full significance a brief outline of the situation and the events which preceded it is necessary.

Detroit at this period is thus described by McMaster: "Detroit alone was worthy to be called a town. The place was founded in 1783, and, except in population, had never taken one step forward since the first hut was put up on the straits. The inhabitants were believed to number three thousand. In language and customs they were French. In religion they were Roman Catholics. In knowledge of the affairs of the world they were extremely ignorant. For a hundred years the farms of precisely the same size had been kept in the same families, and cultivated with the same kind of implements in the same way. The house of each farmer was close to the road, and the road was close to the water's edge. Near each house was an orchard, and in each orchard the same kind of fruit trees were to be seen. Year after year the same crops were raised in the same succession. When a patch of land became exhausted it was suffered to lie fallow. Of the value of manure the farmers knew nothing, and wantonly flung the yield of the barnyard into the waters of the straits. To go to church regularly, to perform their religious duties strictly, to fast, to confess, and to pay their tithes to the priest promptly, was with them the chief duty of man. The priest was the one being on earth to whom they looked up with mingled love and awe. He was their spiritual and their temporal guide. He healed all quarrels and adjusted all disputes. With courts and judges, lawyers and juries, they would have nothing to do. Indeed, the first appearance of such among them was the occasion of an outburst of indignation which was with difficulty soothed. Many resolved to dwell no longer in a land where life and property were at the disposal of godless men, gathered their goods and went over the border to the Canadian side. The town proper was made up of the fort, the battery, and a collection of ugly houses surrounded by a high stockade. The streets were a rod wide, and the inhabitants chiefly engaged in the fur trade. A few went out to the trapping grounds themselves. Others sent out Pawnee Indians whom they had purchased and made slaves."

From Griswold to Cass street, and Larned street to the river was surrounded by a stockade. There were four gates on each side with block houses over each

VIEW OF FORT LERNOULT IN 1796.

Based on a rude contemporary sketch, in possession of C. M. Burton, Esq.

on the east, west and north sides. Each block house had four six-pounders and there were also two batteries of six guns each facing the river. Back of the stockade was Fort Lernoult, which had been erected in 1778 by the orders of Major R. B. Lernoult. It was located between what are now Griswold and Wayne streets, and extended from Lafayette street south of Fort street. It was well designed and thoroughly constructed. Work upon it was prosecuted from November, 1778, without intermission, till after the following March. This fort was no part of the town, but had its entrance toward the town by a passage way underneath the trees with a drawbridge over the ditch. The citadel on what is now the corner of Jefferson avenue and Wayne street, was connected with the fort by a subterranean passage along the route of which was the powder magazine. On each side of the entrance of the fort was an iron twenty-four-pounder, while each side of the fort was defended by two twenty-four-pounders and four cannon were placed at each bastion. The flag staff was in the southwest angle of the fort in the lot where the Owen residence now stands.

The surrender of Lord Cornwallis to Washington in 1781, followed by the preliminary treaty of peace between Great Britain and the United States, agreed upon at Paris, November 30th, 1782, theoretically determined the boundaries of the new republic. The thirteen British colonies in North America, which had thus become the thirteen United States of North America, represented clear and definite ideas, politically and socially, but the boundaries of the territory were only vaguely determined. The United States described in the instructions to John Adams in 1779, was quite a different country geographically from the same United States whose independence was acknowledged in Paris in 1782. Neither England nor Spain regarded the treaty of Paris as finally settling the destiny of the country of the United States west of the mountains.

Although that grand prologue to the constitution and forerunner of national emancipation, the ordinance of 1787, proclaimed eternal freedom for the northwest territory, its boundaries were indefinite, and it had not yet been surrendered by the British. While in the treaty of Paris in 1782, His Britannic Majesty promised, among other things, "to withdraw all his armies, garrisons and fleets from said United States, and from every post, place and harbor within the same, with all convenient speed," there was still left unsettled a question of territory larger than the one which brought on the French and Indian war in 1754. In addition to this indefiniteness of boundary, the relation between the new government and the former colonies, now matured into states, was novel and peculiar, and their respective rights over this territory not yet determined.

In the beginning the government of the United States was distinctly federal rather than national, and large portions of the territory of the northwest were within the original boundaries of the respective colonies and were claimed to have passed to them when they were erected into states. At the same time France was provoked by the treaties entered into by the United States with England and Spain, and looked with longing eyes upon these vast possessions which less than half a century before had been wrested from her by Great Britain. Most of the settlers in the territory were English or French. The posts were the depots or stations of the increasingly lucrative fur trade, so desirable in the minds of Europeans. These considerations and the very natural desire of

England to interpose between her possessions in America and the new United States a territory of neutral ground fairly in the hands of the savages—constituting a "buffer state" between the United States and Canada—were the real reasons for the unjustifiable delay in carrying out the treaty, and with all convenient speed "withdrawing the British armies, garrisons and fleets from the United States and every post, place and harbor within the same." While England attempted to justify this delay upon the ground that the United States had on their part violated their promises in the treaty, these claims were completely refuted by Jefferson, then Secretary of State in 1793, in his correspondence with Mr. Hammond, the envoy extraordinary of Great Britain. Whatever may have been the true cause of the delay, the result was, that for thirteen years the northwestern posts "were sharp thorns in the sides of the United States." Exhausting as had been the War of the Revolution to the young nation, it was compelled to continue an harassing Indian war, that only ceased with the brilliant victory of General Wayne at the battle of the Fallen Timbers in 1794.

In July, 1783, the request of Washington, through Baron Steuben, for a transfer of possession of Detroit, Mackinac and Oswego, and the minor posts, was met with an insolent refusal on the part of General Haldiman, the British commander in Canada.

In the following year General William Hull was sent, with the approval of Congress, to induce Haldiman to give up the post, but he met with a like refusal.

In 1786, President Adams, then minister to England, informed Congress that he had made a demand for the western posts, and had been refused on the stale pretense, so conclusively answered by Jefferson, that many of the states had violated the treaty in regard to payment of British debts.

Matters were further complicated by the active efforts of Dr. John Connolly, a Virginian tory, to induce the Kentucky settlers to take sides with the English, with the purpose of wresting Louisiana from Spain, and securing the free navigation of the Mississippi. In 1787 and 1788, he was in Detroit a considerable portion of the time. The English settlers urged the retention of Detroit, and in June, 1787, the garrison was re-enforced by a full regiment and two companies, making a force of more than two regiments. In pursuance of the plan to hold the post, Lord Dorchester personally visited Detroit in 1788, and, under his directions, the town was doubly picketed, and other defensive works erected. In 1790, John Knox, then United States Secretary-of-War, wrote to Governor St. Clair, that it was reported that Benedict Arnold was in Detroit about the first of June, and that he had reviewed the militia there. In the same year President Washington, who, with clear foresight, very soon after the treaty of 1782, had prophesied "that England would retain the posts as long as they could be held under any pretense whatever," communicated to his cabinet his apprehensions that Lord Dorchester contemplated sending an expedition from Detroit against Louisiana. Meantime the Indians had grown increasingly hostile under the encouragement of the British.

In 1786 a grand confederate council of the Indians northwest of the Ohio was held at the mouth of the Detroit River. It was attended by the Six Nations, the Hurons, Ottawas, Maumees, Shawnees, Chippewas, Cherokees, Delawares, Pottawattamies, and the confederates of the Wabash. The question of difference was one of boundary. The Indians insisted that the Americans should not cross the Ohio River, but there was no intimation of war, provided the United States did not encroach on the Indian land. While there was a treaty between Great Britain and the United States concerning this territory, the Indians were not included in it, and the savages complained that the United States would "kindle the council fires wherever they thought proper without consulting the Indians." Closely following this council, the Hurons of Detroit sent a message, sealed with strings of wampum, to the Five Nations, complaining of the delay of the Americans in answering their message, and desiring the Five Nations "to be strong and punctual of your promises to be with us early and in time." As an evidence of the intimate relations between the British and the Indians, an account of the proceedings of this council was forwarded to Lord Dorchester.

In 1791 Canada was divided into an upper and lower province, the former being placed under the administration of Col. T. S. Simcoe, who established his headquarters as governor of the newly organized territory at Niagara. He, with the British agents, Col. McKee, Capt. Elliott and the notorious Simon Girty, threw all their influence against the United States, and it is affirmed that Lord Dorchester assisted their efforts by a speech to the Seven Nations of Canada, as well as all the other Indians at the grand council. Governor Simcoe proceeded to Detroit, and thence, with a strong detachment, to the foot of the Miami Rapids, where he erected a fortress. Undoubtedly his fort was built primarily to defend Detroit. It was, in fact, the re-occupation of a position held by the British during the latter part of the Revolution, the evacuation of which had been bad policy.

During the whole period, Detroit was the theatre of its most interesting councils. It was represented by the half-breeds of the place to the savages around the post, and also to remote tribes, that Governor Simcoe was to march to their aid with fifteen hundred men; that he was giving clothing and all necessary supplies; that all the speeches sent to them were red as blood; the wampum and the feathers, the war pipes and the hatchets, and even the tobacco was painted red. At one time Alexander McKenzie, an agent of the British government, was employed to paint himself as an Indian, and he convened a grand council at Detroit, exhibiting himself with pipes and wampum as the credentials of his authority.

Elliott and the other British residents addressed the council, stating that McKenzie was an ambassador who had returned from the remote tribes of the upper lakes and that their bands were armed with the tomahawk and scalping knife and were ready to fall upon the Americans, and that the savages upon the banks of the Mississippi were prepared to descend and attack the settlements of Virginia and Ohio. McKenzie spoke the Indian language with fluency and preserved his character to the life. He was aided in his deception by some of the Wyandottes and Shawnees, who were acquainted with his secret and in the conspiracy. These means brought into the field against the United States, the Ottawas, the Miamis, the Pottawattamies, the Delawares, the Shawnees, the Chippewas, and the Seven Nations of Canada. Many of the French traders at Detroit and in Michigan, induced by the fear that if they did not join the Indian cause they would not be permitted to trade with the Indians in their own territory, took up arms against the United States. Thus the United States was met on the one hand with the refusal of Great Britain to yield up the posts, and on the other with the organized and armed opposition of the savages to any interferences with the territory which they claimed as their own.

Peaceable negotiations with the Indians who had gradually strengthened into a confederation of tribes throughout the western forests was attempted but without success. General Harmar with a force of fourteen hundred men was then sent to subdue the savages. He succeeded in destroying and laying waste many of their villages and fields, but his advance was checked near Chillicothe, Ohio, where he was defeated in October, 1790, with great slaughter. After his defeat the Indians daily paraded the streets of Detroit, exhibiting in triumph the scalps of American soldiers.

In 1792 Governor St. Clair succeeded in command and marched into the wilderness with an army of two thousand men. He was surprised near the Miami villages by the Indians under the command of Little Turtle, and notwithstanding his great personal gallantry in his efforts to rally his retreating forces, he was forced to retreat with very heavy loss.

These successive repulses aroused Congress to a vigorous prosecution of the war, and General Anthony Wayne was put in command of the forces. His fame in the Revolutionary War had preceded him, and the Indians feared him. They credited him not only with bravery to rashness but with much stratagem and cunning, and named him the Black Snake. He proceeded with characteristic energy. In the latter part of 1793, he erected a stockade on the site of St. Clair's defeat, which he called Fort Recovery, and having fully matured his plans, on the 4th of July, 1794 followed the savages into the depths of the wilderness. Cautiously moving down the left bank of the Maumee, he reached the rapids about the 19th of August, and erected a small work called Fort Deposit, about four miles above the British post. He found the Indians entrenched under the very shadow of the English fort, which had been fortified not long before by a force sent from Detroit. General Wayne, therefore, prepared himself to act defensively against both civilized and savage foe. His army amounted to about three thousand men. Opposed to him was the Indian league which extended throughout the whole northwestern frontier.

On the 30th August, 1794, he attacked the savages.

His plan of battle was to send forward a battalion of mounted riflemen with instructions if attacked, to retreat in apparent confusion in order to entice the savages into a less advantageous position, and upon concerted signals to turn with his infantry, which included the renowned Wayne legion, the right flank of the enemy. But the day was rainy, the signals from the drums could not be distinctly heard and the plan was not wholly executed. His victory, however, was complete. After a stubborn resistance, the savages were defeated and fled to the very walls of Fort Miami. The battle is known in history as the battle of the Fallen Timbers. After the Indians had retreated, General Wayne devastated their fields and burned their buildings, among them the house of Col. McKee. While he had defeated the Indians he did not know how soon he must defend himself against an attack by the British from the fort, but in the crisis the doughty warrior never flinched. He proudly paraded his army in front of the fort and although he saw the British gunners standing at their guns with lighted matches in their hands, eagerly awaiting the order to fire, he rode forward with his staff to the very battlements and reconnoitered the position with the utmost deliberation. No attack was made upon him and he advanced by easy marches toward Fort Defiance, destroying the Indian cornfields on the bottom lands of the Maumee, then proceeded up the Maumee River and built Fort Wayne.

There is no doubt that in this battle a detachment of militia from Detroit were associated and fought with the Indians, General Wayne in his official report describes the enemy "a combined force of the hostile Indians and a considerable number of the volunteers and militia of Detroit." A Mr. Smith, clerk of the court at Detroit, was killed in the action at the head of a company which fought against the Americans.

It was estimated that thirteen hundred Indians fled to Detroit for British protection after the battle. In the fall of that year Governor Simcoe approved of the provision of an extra surgeon and another hospital and made extensive preparations to strengthen the post at Detroit. Fort Lernoult was newly fortified, a new block house erected, and six boats ordered to be built at Chatham. Simcoe still encouraged the Indians. He told them that Ohio was their right and title and that he had given orders to the commandant at Fort Miami to fire on the Americans when they made their appearance again, but the Indians had been severely punished by General Wayne and were distrustful of the ability of the English to protect them. The battle of the Fallen Timbers ended all the Indian hostilities for the time being and was followed in the next year by the treaty of Greenville. Before this, and almost contemporaneous with Wayne's victory, Jay's admirable diplomacy had accomplished the treaty of 1794 which bears his name, under which England bound herself to deliver up the northwestern posts.

The treaty called for the surrender of the post by the British on June 1st, 1796, but the order to evacuate was not given until June 2d. It was dated at Quebec and signed by George Beckwith, adjutant general.

On the 7th day of July, 1796, General Hamtramck sent on to Detroit two small vessels from Fort Miami with a detachment of artillery and infantry consisting of sixty-five men, together with a number of cannon with ammunition, etc., under the command of Captain Moses Porter. Upon his arrival on the 11th of July, the British troops, under the command of Col. Richard England, evacuated the town. The Union Jack was hauled down, Old Glory floated on the breeze, and Detroit was free.

Under the benign influence of the constitution and the incomparable privileges of the ordinance of 1787, the little post of 3,000 souls has grown in a single century to a superb and peerless city, and the wilderness of the northwest is jeweled with the happy homes of millions of freemen.

THE ORATION.
BY HON. JULIUS C. BURROWS.

Fellow Citizens—That patriotic impulse which prompts the people to search out, preserve, dedicate, and fittingly mark, with tablet or monument, the places of historic interest along the highway of a nation's course, made memorable by the happening of some important event in the history of the country, is a spirit deserving the highest commendation. It is prompted by and serves a double purpose. It not only pays a fitting tribute to the memory of the actors in such events, but it serves, for all times, as an inspiration to the passing generations. We may read, unmoved, the story of the Pilgrim Fathers, or the history of the Declaration of Independence, but we cannot stand on Plymouth Rock, or within the shadow of Independence Hall, without feeling a quicker heart-throb, and being imbued with something of that spirit of devotion to the cause of civil and religious liberty, which inspired the men and women who made these places immortal. I regard, therefore, every step taken toward the preservation of these landmarks of history as most auspicious omens.

And here I pause to say that public acknowledgment ought to be made to those patriotic orders, in the United States, engaged to-day in the laudable undertaking of rescuing from oblivion and preserving from desecration, places made historic by the events which there transpired. They are not only writing history, but they are doing that which will exert a silent, yet potent, influence on all the generations to come. In this spirit, and with this purpose, we mark to-day a spot of historic interest, not only to the state, but to the nation. In recognition of the importance of the event, the Congress of the United States co-operates in the designating and preserving of the place which will be forever memorable in the annals of our country.

Here it was, a hundred years ago, that the British flag gave way to the banner of the republic, and the Stars and Stripes were unfurled in token of the sovereignty of the United States. I have neither the time, nor is this the occasion, to rehearse the story of the struggle of the colonies for national independence. It is sufficient for my purpose to-day to say that the termination of the War of the Revolution found the British government in possession of the military posts on the western frontiers, among the most important of which was that at Detroit, which she had occupied since the French relinquished their claim to the territory in 1760. The seat of war for national independence being chiefly confined within the limits of the colonies participating in the struggle, England was permitted to hold these outlying posts practically undisturbed, which she used as recruiting stations for her Indian allies, whom she invited into her service, and whom she subsequently employed to harass the settlers on the frontier, and impede, if not prevent, the settlement of the northwest territory.

These points were too remote, and the forces holding them too insignificant to engage the attention of the Continental army. By the terms of the treaty of peace, however, between Great Britain and the United States, concluded in 1783, it was expressly stipulated and agreed that "His Britannic Majesty shall with all convenient speed, and without causing any destruction of property, or carrying away any negroes or other property of the American inhabitants, withdraw all his armies, garrisons and fleets from the United States, and from every part, place and harbor within the same."

A strict compliance with the terms of this treaty, imposed upon Great Britain the obligation to withdraw her military forces from every portion of the territory of the United States and abandon all assumption of power over any part of their domain.

It is a matter of history, however, that the British government, while conforming to the terms of the treaty within the limits of the states, persisted for a period of nearly thirteen years thereafter in retaining possession of the posts on the frontier, including that of Detroit, and in exercising authority and asserting dominion over an extensive territory in the northwest.

After the close of the war, and during the entire period of the existence of the government of the confederation, and prolonged under the national constitution of 1787, even until near the close of Washington's second administration as President of the United States, the British flag continued to float over a British garrison quartered within the limits of this city. To us of to-day, removed by more than a century of time from these startling events, it seems incredible that the British government should have been permitted to have asserted and maintained even a show of authority over any portion of the territory of the United States. Circumstances, however, contributed to this assumption of power, and rendered its exercise comparatively safe. The country had just emerged from a protracted and exhaustive struggle for independence and found itself with a bankrupt treasury and a ruined credit. The government of the confederation set up in 1781, and continued until 1789, was too feeble to command confidence at home or respect abroad, and was powerless to assert itself even within the limits of the confederated states.

It has been well said, "The Continental Congress, under the articles of confederation, may make and conclude treaties, but can only recommend the observance of them. They may appoint ambassadors, but they cannot defray even the expenses of their table. They may borrow money in their own name on the faith of the union, but they cannot pay a dollar. They may coin money, but they cannot import an ounce of bullion. They may make war and determine the number of troops necessary to carry it on, but they are powerless to raise a single soldier. In short, they may declare everything, but they can do nothing."

Such was the character of the government set up during the struggle for independence, and permitted to continue until the 4th of March, 1789. It is not surprising, therefore, that Great Britain, in the continued occupancy of these western posts, after the treaty of 1783, should be wholly indifferent to the wishes or existence of a government rapidly falling into decay, and should be actuated in her course solely by considerations of personal interest.

What these considerations were which prompted the retention of these posts, history fails fully to disclose; but that they were inimical to the interests of the United States does not admit of question. It is not improbable that considerations of trade, to the promotion of which Great Britain is always keenly alive, was the mainspring of her action, and it is barely possible she may have indulged the hope, if not the expectation, that the experiment of free government in the new world, as exemplified in the confederation, was doomed to a speedy and disastrous issue, in which event, by the retention of her foothold on the western frontier, she would be in a position to regain her power and reassert her sovereignty.

Whatever may be the truth of the matter, either of these considerations would have been sufficient to influence her judgment and determine her course; but it is more than probable that the importance of her trade with the northwest, which in 1785, in furs alone, is said to have reached the magnitude of one hundred and eighty thousand pounds annually, coupled with the advantages of an enlarged market for British goods, to which consideration she is never indifferent, was the primary, if not the controlling motive for the retention of these frontier posts.

The question of promoting British trade and British interest would seem to have been uppermost in the minds of the representatives of the English government, when every application for permission to build or navigate private vessels on the lakes was refused, and the recommendations made to the home government as late as 1785, "That a sufficient number of the queen's ships be kept upon the lakes to do the carrying trade and that all other crafts whatever be prohibited."

But whatever the motive, whether trade or territorial retention or acquisition, the fact remains that when shortly after the treaty of peace a demand was made for the surrender of this and other points in the northwest, the request was flatly refused and the occupancy continued. This could be done with impunity, for there was not sufficient vitality remaining in the old government of the confederation to effectively assert the rights of the people, or enforce the mandates of the government. Fortunately for the inhabitants of the United States, doubly fortunate for the cause of human liberty and free government, the rotten fabric of confederation speedily gave way to the substitution and enduring structure of

1787, under and by virtue of which a national government was inaugurated, possessed of ample power, not only to maintain its own existence, but to enforce obedience to its rightful demands. Yet even then British occupancy continued. It seems incredible that for more than seven years after the establishment of the national government, and the inauguration of Washington as President of the United States, the British flag continued to float above the posts of the western frontier.

When we consider, however, the difficulties attending the inauguration of a new government, the exhausted resources of the people just emerging from a protracted war, perplexed by a burdensome debt, a doubtful credit, it is not surprising that the authorities were slow to take any step which might provoke a renewal of hostilities and involve the new government in the wastes and uncertainties of war. Time and diplomacy might be relied upon to accomplish the desired end. The continued occupancy, however, by the British, of these strongholds on the western frontier, was not only a flagrant usurpation of authority, but was characterized by a spirit of animosity, which made their retention peculiarly exasperating and offensive.

Not content during the War of the Revolution, with invoking the aid of her savage allies, now, when the war was concluded and peace declared, Great Britain sought by every means at her command to create, foster and perpetuate a spirit of hostility among the Indians of the northwest towards the hardy frontiersmen pushing their settlements across the Ohio. To this end they encouraged the Indians to insist upon the Ohio River as the southern boundary of their possessions, to decline to enter into any treaty with the United States touching these lands, and were made to believe that the English government in retaining the posts, was actuated only by a desire to protect the Indians in the rightful possession of their territory. It was an English Indian superintendent, Johnson, who said to the Indians, "It is for your sakes, chiefly, if not entirely, that we hold these forts."

Lord Dorchester, speaking through Capt. Matthews, whom he sent to command at Detroit in 1786, after ex_____ ,- ing regret that the Indians had consented to p__ ... the Americans to construct a road to Niagara, said to them : "In the future, His Lordship wishes you to act as is best for your interests. He cannot begin a war with the Americans because some of their people encroach and make depredations upon parts of the Indian country ; but they must see it is His Lordship's intention to defend the posts, and that while they are preserved, the Indians must feel great security therefrom, and consequently the Americans greater difficulty in taking possession of their land. But should they once become masters of the posts, they will surround the Indians, and accomplish their purpose with little trouble. You seem apprehensive that the English are not very anxious about the defense of the posts. You will soon be satisfied that they have nothing more at heart, provided that it continues to be the wish of the Indians, and that they remain firm in doing their part of the business, by preventing the Americans from coming into their country, and consequently, from marching to the posts. On the other hand, if the Indians think it more for their interest that the Americans should have possession of the posts, and be established in their country, they ought to declare it, that the English need no longer be put to the vast and unnecessary expense and inconveniences of keeping the posts, the chief object of which is to protect their Indian allies, and the loyalists who have suffered with them."

This artful pronunciamento was well calculated, as it was evidently designed, to encourage the Indians to persist in their claim of territorial jurisdiction, and incite them to fresh acts of hostility against the venturesome pioneer. With such assurances of friendship and support, backed by the presence of the British garrisons, and the sight of the British flag, it is not to be wondered at that the Indians were encouraged to persist in their hostility towards the United States, and that all efforts to secure possession of this territory by peaceful instrumentality proved wholly abortive.

The defeat of the forces of Gen. Harmer, sent against the Indians in 1790, followed a year later by the defeat of St. Clair, served to increase their hostility, and demonstrated how thoroughly British influence aroused and solidified the Indians in defense of what they had been taught and encouraged to believe were their inalienable rights. Brant, the chief of the Six Nations, whose influence was solicited by President Washington, after the defeat of Harmer and St. Clair, to bring about a peace with the western tribe, to which end a commission was appointed on the part of the United States in 1793, in explanation of the failure of such commission, did not hesitate to declare it was British influence which prevented its consummation. "To our surprise," he said, "when upon the point of entering upon a treaty, with the commissioners, we found it was opposed by those acting under the British government, and hope of assistance was given to our western brethren to encourage them to insist upon the Ohio as the boundary between them and the United States."

The response of the Indians to the overtures of this commission disclosed the "power behind the throne," when they declared: "We desire you to consider that our only demand is the peaceable possession of a small part of our once great country. We shall be persuaded that you mean to do us justice if you agree that the Ohio River shall remain the boundary between us."

I have said this much in explanation of the motive for the retention of the posts on the frontier. Thus ended this renewed effort on the part of the government to conciliate the Indians, and establish, by treaty stipulation, the peace and security of the border.

The Indians elated with the victories over Harmer and St. Clair, were emboldened in their manifestations of hostility, while the governor of Canada proceeded to erect a new fort on the banks of the Maumee, which was interpreted by the Indians as a fresh assurance of sympathy and support. This attempt on the part of the British to entrench themselves more securely on the border, was declared by Washington to be the most daring act yet committed by the British agents in America, though not the most hostile or cruel, for he declared: "There does not remain a doubt in the mind of any well-informed person in this country, not shut against conviction, that the murders of our helpless women and innocent children, along our frontiers, result from the conduct of the agents of Great Britain in this country."

With increased hostility on the part of the Indians, and a fresh assumption of power on the part of Great Britain; it was manifest affairs were rapidly approaching a crisis, when it would become necessary for the government to assert its rightful dominion and admonish the Indians and their British allies, that the savagery of the one and the domination of the other could not longer be tolerated. To this end Gen. Wayne, in command of the United States forces, entered the territory on the 20th of August, 1794, fought a bloody but decisive battle with the Indians within hearing of the newly erected British fort on the Maumee. The officer in command of the fort, Maj. Campbell, having inquired of Gen. Wayne what interpretation was to be placed upon the near approach of his command to the garrison which he had the honor to command, must have received the impression from the general's reply that it was none of the major's particular business, as he said: "The most full and satisfactory answer was given the day before from the muzzle of my guns in an action with a horde of savages in the vicinity of the fort, and which terminated gloriously to the American arms." And the general took occasion to add, for the information of the British commandant, which must have served as food for reflection, that, "Had the battle continued until the Indians were driven under the influence of your fort and guns, they would not much have impeded the progress of the victorious army under my command."

It was the beginning of the end. In spite of the efforts of British emissaries to induce the Indians to prolong the conflict, on the 3d of August, 1795, the Indians responded to the invitation of Gen. Wayne to meet him in council, at Greenville, where they entered into and concluded a treaty of peace. By the terms of this treaty extensive grants of land were ceded to the United States, among them a strip six miles wide on the eastern shore of Michigan from the Raisin River to Lake St. Clair, and all claims to the posts at Detroit and Mackinac wholly surrendered. In the meantime a treaty had been concluded with Great Britain, by which it was stipulated among other things, that "on or before the 1st day of June, 1796, the British garrison should be withdrawn from all posts and places within the limits of the United States."

The execution of the terms of this treaty was somewhat delayed, but on the 11th day of July, 1796, a hundred years ago this very day, the American flag was for the first time unfurled at Detroit, proclaiming the departure of an alien power and the ascended sovereignty of the United States. It is most fitting, therefore, that the centennial anniversary of that day should be commemorated on the very spot made memorable by the happening of this great event and that it should be marked with enduring tablet that the memory of it may be preserved and transmitted to those who are to come after us.

And let me say in this connection, that what occurred here a century ago to-day, was fraught with more than local interest. It meant the enforcement of that great ordinance of 1787 which, for wise statesmanship and patriotic purpose, is entitled to hold a place in American history second only to the Declaration of Independence. For it was by this ordinance that the territory northwest of the Ohio, embraced within the present limits of the states of Ohio, Indiana, Illinois, Wisconsin and Michigan, was set apart and forever dedicated to free government and enlightened citizenship.

It guaranteed freedom of religious worship, a comprehensive bill of rights, encouragement of schools, that the states to be formed from this territory not less than three nor more than five should remain permanently in the confederacy, and finally that there should be neither slavery nor involuntary servitude within the limits of said territory, except in the punishment of crime, of which the party shall have been duly convicted.

By this ordinance the great northwest was made the nursery of civil and religious liberty—the cradle of free states and free men. And what was of incalculable value, as subsequent events demonstrated, its terms were to remain forever unalterable, except by common consent. Every attempt to abrogate or suspend its provisions proved wholly abortive. This great ordinance, irrevocable in character, defended by resolute and uncompromising men, proved to be an insurmountable barrier to the extension of slavery in the northwest, and a wall of defense to the champions of free states and free men.

We do well, therefore, to commemorate an event which is not only of local interest, but which, in its far-reaching influence, has been felt through the intervening years, and made its lasting impress on the century. The flag which a hundred years ago was here unfurled, on the then borders of civilization, proclaiming the sovereignty of the nation over the northwest, has been borne across and subdued a continent, and floats to-day, with augmented power and glory, over seventy-five millions of people, possessing a domain imperial in extent, and a government securely reposing on the public will.

May that banner, symbolizing unity and liberty, float on forever, commanding the allegiance of the citizen and the respect of mankind.

Senator Burrows' oration was enthusiastically applauded.

JAMES B. ANGELL, LL. D.,
President of the University of Michigan.

PRESIDENT ANGELL'S ADDRESS.

Pres. James B. Angell, of the University of Michigan, was then called upon by the chairman, for a few words. He was received with hearty cheers, and spoke as follows:

Mr. President, Ladies and Gentlemen—He must be a bolder or a vainer man than I am, who can willingly rise to his feet here, to speak at this late hour, and to follow the two distinguished men, whose instructive and eloquent addresses we have listened to with such delight. But I remember that Gen. Alger is in command, and whenever he has faced a foe, it has proved useless to resist. And, indeed, it is not easy to keep silent, when one stands in this inspiring presence, and on this sacred spot, and surrounded by these precious relics of the past.

Rhode Islander as I am by birth, I cannot, unmoved, take in my hand this telescope, which that brave Rhode Islander, Oliver Hazard Perry, captured from the ship of the British commander, in the decisive battle of Lake Erie, and he must have a colder heart than I, who can lay his hand on this old flag staff without feeling something of the touch of patriotic joy with which those sixty-five brave American soldiers saw the Stars and Stripes raised to its peak a hundred years ago this day, in token of the establishment of our sovereignty over the whole northwest.

It was a happy thought to celebrate this day. I have often wondered that Detroit has not given more opportunities to commemorate the great men and the great events in its remarkable history. Long years ago, the sagacious men, who laboriously ascended this stream, saw that this place was "beautiful for situation, the joy of the whole earth," that here was sure to be a city, "the Queen of the Straits," wearing at her girdle the key to the upper lakes, and to the great northwest. You make pilgrimages to Bunker Hill, to Valley Forge, and to Yorktown, as to sacred shrines. But to what spot in all this land are more romantic and thrilling historic associations attached than to this, when one recalls the adventures of the old explorers and missionaries, the gifted men who administered affairs under the French rule ; the shrewd English administrators and soldiers who succeeded them ; the Indian wars, which centered here ; the painful events of the Revolutionary days, and of the War of 1812. Our children and our children's children should all be made to feel, by celebrations like this, and by historic monuments and commemorative tablets, that here, at their own homes, is a spot as sacred in their country's history, as any in all our broad domain.

The distinguished speakers who have preceded me have suggested, and truly, that one of the reasons why Great Britain retained this and other frontier posts for thirteen years after the Treaty of Independence, was their doubt whether we were really going to be able to retain our independence. Under the weakness of our old confederation this doubt on the part of the English was perhaps not unreasonable. But, may I call your attention to the more surprising fact that long after the establishment of our stronger government under the constitution, the English seemed to cherish the same doubt. In 1814, at the opening of the negotiations for the Treaty of Ghent, the very first proposition made by the British commissioners to ours, and made as a *sine qua non* of the treaty, was that we should set apart for Indians the vast territory now comprising the states of Michigan, Wisconsin, Illinois, and a considerable part of the states of Indiana and Ohio, and that we should never purchase it from them. A sort of Indian sovereignty under British guaranty was to be established in our domain. Coupled with this was a demand that we should have no armed force on the lakes. There were other demands scarcely less preposterous. Think of making such "cheeky" demands as these to John Quincy Adams and Henry Clay and James A. Bayard and Albert Gallatin and Jonathan Russell. It did not take these spirited men many minutes to send back answer in effect that until the United States had lost all sense of independence, they would not even listen to such propositions. They threatened to go home. Castlereagh, the Prime Minister, happening to reach Ghent on his way to Vienna, ordered an abatement of the British demands, and so an honorable peace was made. But the same idea of a "buffer state" of Indians under British influence, to be used in need as a means of regaining power here, was cherished at the outset as was entertained in 1790.

And even if we come down to our Civil War, who has forgotten how Lord John Russell, in response to our demands for the suppression of cruisers like the Alabama, replied that Great Britain had no municipal law which forbade the construction of such vessels, and refused to consider our contention that international law called for the prohibition of them. He did not believe that we were to survive as a nation long enough or strong enough to enforce our demands. He afterwards manfully confessed his mistake. But his first answer to us afterwards cost England fifteen and a half million dollars. And did not Hon. Mr. Gladstone declare that Mr. Jefferson Davis had created a nation? With all our respect for him, it is hard for us to forget that unhappy remark, which he had no business to make.

But, thank God, when the brave veterans at Appomattox struck the last fatal blow and ended the war of secession, you also won a victory of which perhaps you little thought at the time you slew the last lingering doubt in the English mind of the ability and will of this nation to maintain its integrity and its independence. From that day to this no Englishman has raised the question whether we are to remain a mighty and free nation.

But I say all this without any spark of bitterness toward England. Thank God, when her troops quitted our soil they did not take away with them those muniments of liberty, which we brought from the home of our fathers, the habeas corpus, the right of trial by jury, the right of petition, the spirit of obedience to law, the inextinguishable love of civil and religious liberty. These English-speaking races, now that England recognizes thoroughly our independence and our strength, bound together by the ties of a common language, common blood, similar laws and political institutions, fondly hope to settle all their misunderstandings without war, and by their example of good government, to commend free institutions to all nations.

The whole world respects us now. There is no sea so remote, and no pathway of the traveler so excluded, that the flag of our Union is not there sufficient protection to the humblest American citizen. And it is to you, brave old veterans of the war, that we owe this proud position of our nation.

When the applause which greeted the speaker had subsided, a benediction was pronounced by Rt. Rev. John S. Foley, D. D., Roman Catholic Bishop of Detroit, after which the great gathering dispersed.

THE LUNCH ON THE RIVER.

Immediately after leaving the hall, the speakers and distinguished visitors were driven to the foot of Woodward avenue, where the steamer Pleasure was awaiting them. About 300, including the committees of the day and the members of the Fourth Infantry, M. N. G., who had acted as ushers at the hall, boarded the vessel and were carried several miles down the river. An excellent lunch was served, and Haug's mandolin orchestra enlivened the occasion with music. There was no set programme, but conversation and music made the time pass very pleasantly. The day was fine and nothing could have been wished to add to the perfect enjoyment of the occasion.

THE MILITARY PARADE.

Between the hours of four and six in the afternoon the celebration took the form of a grand military parade. Major Ford H. Rogers was chief marshal and Gen. Arthur Bresler chief of staff. The parade formed on Jefferson avenue at Dequindre street, and the route of march was down Jefferson to Woodward, up Woodward and Monroe avenues to Miami avenue, thence up to the Grand Circus and back by Woodward to Michigan avenue; thence by Wayne street to Lafayette avenue, to Third street, to Fort street and by that thoroughfare to the Campus Martius, where the various companies and organizations participating were disbanded. Forty-five minutes were consumed in passing a given point.

On the Fort street side of the new Federal Building, to the east of the main entrance, a reviewing stand had been erected, where the members of the executive committee, the invited guests and the members of the city government occupied seats.

On the entire line of march the sidewalks were thronged by tens of thousands of spectators. The buildings on the route were gaily decorated and every window was filled with heads. All along the route the enthusiasm was as great as the crowds.

The parade was led by a detachment of mounted police followed by the entire force under the command of Chief Starkweather. Then in order:

The chief marshal and his aides.

The 19th Infantry U. S. A., with its band, Col. Snyder leading in person.

Gov. John T. Rich, in citizen's clothes, riding on a black horse, and attended by his staff, mounted and in full uniform.

The 4th Infantry Michigan National Guard, with its band.

A battalion of the Michigan Naval Reserve, in naval uniform.

A small detachment of the Detroit Light Guard Veteran Corps.

The second division, under command of Capt. John Conline, U. S. A., was made up of

Parke, Davis & Co.'s Band.
Detroit Post No. 384, G. A. R.
Fairbanks Post, No. 17, G. A. R.
Farquahar Post No. 152, G. A. R.
Michigan Post No. 393, G. A. R.

A body of the Union Veterans' Union.

A party of 21 little girls, in patriotic colors, carrying red, white and blue umbrellas.

Ten colored veterans.

The second division was completed by the "living flag"—a body of 250 girls and boys dressed in white, blue or red clothes throughout, and so disposed that when looked down upon from any height the phalanx presented an exact representation of the American flag.

The third division, under Assistant Marshal A. P. T. Beniteau, embraced:

The Detroit Guardmen's Band.
The Maybury Cadets.
The Detroit Catholic Cadets.
The Detroit Catholic Grays.
The St. Elizabeth's Catholic Cadets.
The St. John's Catholic Cadets.
The St. Boniface Cadets.
The Detroit Catholic Rifles.
The St. Paul's Cadets, (St. Casimir's Parish).
The Kosciusko Guards.
St. Michael's Commandery.
St. Ladislaus Commandery.
St. Stanislaus Commandery.

All the cadets were uniformed and armed, and attracted attention by their excellent drill.

The fourth division, under Col. Fred. E. Farnsworth, was made up as follows:

The Metropolitan Band.
Knights of St. John and Patriarchs Militant.
The Elks, in white uniforms and white umbrellas.

The fifth division was marshaled by Ralph Phelps, assisted by Col. R. G. Butler. It included:

The two Newsboys' Bands.

The Letter Carriers in uniform and admirably drilled.

The Fire and Police Notification Company.

The Newsboys' Association.

It was six o'clock when the parade terminated and the exercises of the day were at an end.

LETTERS OF REGRET.

Letters of regret were received from Governors Busiel, of New Hampshire; Woodbury, of Vermont; Coffin, of Connecticut; Morton, of New York; Griggs, of New Jersey; O'Ferrall, of Virginia; Carr, of North Carolina; Atkinson, of Georgia; McCorkle, of West Virginia; Bradley, of Kentucky; Foster, of Louisiana; Stone, of Missouri; Altgeld, of Illinois; Matthews, of Indiana; Bushnell, of Ohio; Cullen, of Texas; Thornton, of New Mexico; Rickards, of Montana, and Lord, of Oregon.

Also from President Cleveland, Postmaster-General Wilson, Secretary of State Olney, Secretary of the Navy Herbert, Attorney-General Harmon, and Justices Brewer, Peckham and Fuller of the Supreme Court, also the French and Russian Ambassadors, Senators Sherman, Vilas, Frye, Allison and McMillan, and Representatives Reed, Fischer and Henderson, and many others.

LETTER FROM GOVERNOR O'FERRALL.

Governor Charles T. O'Ferrall, of Virginia, who had expected to attend the festivities, with his entire staff, was unavoidably prevented. The following letter was received from him:

COMMONWEALTH OF VIRGINIA,
GOVERNOR'S OFFICE.

RICHMOND, VA., July 8th, 1896.

My Dear Mr. Dickinson:

I regret exceedingly I cannot attend De... great celebration. An official engagement over which I have no control will prevent. Our statute requires the board of public works, of which the governor is *ex-officio* president, to assess during the present week the railroads of the state for purposes of taxation, and the board is now engaged in the performance of this important duty.

I beg to assure the good people of your historic city I would be more than happy to be with them, and that I appreciate beyond measure the high compliment they have paid this old commonwealth in their cordial invitation to me as her governor, to be present and address them upon the interesting occasion.

Virginia reciprocates warmly their kind and generous consideration, and her people are more than gratified to find in their hearty action unmistakable evidence that all feelings of estrangement resulting from civil strife have been forever buried, and the two sections stand together in soul and spirit, under one flag and one constitution. Each section has memories which she will ever cherish with peculiar tenderness, yet they are in fact common memories, for they spring from the glories of the American soldier whether he fell under the stars and stripes or the stars and bars. I speak for the South when I say she is as loyal to the flag of our reunited country as she was to the southern cross, and that her sons will be ready at all times to stand shoulder to shoulder with their northern brethren in the maintenance of their country's honor and the defense of their country's rights.

This old dominion State, immortalized in song and story, crowned with glories and hung with memories, and who gave to the cause of republican liberty her Henry, Jefferson, Washington and

Madison, joins with your great State in commemorating "the closing act of the war of American independence."

In conclusion, I beg to again assure you that I regret more than I can express, my inability to be absent from my post at this time. I am indeed almost selfish enough to wish that I could change the date of the evacuation as recorded by the chronicler, and make it a little later, so that I might participate in celebrating the memorable event and meeting with your sturdy northwest people.

Yours very sincerely,
CHAS. T. O'FERRALL.

Hon. Don M. Dickinson, Detroit, Mich.

FROM GOVERNOR MATTHEWS.

EXECUTIVE DEPARTMENT.
INDIANAPOLIS, IND.

July 6th, 1896.

Hon. Don M. Dickinson, Chairman Committee on Invitations, Detroit, Michigan:

DEAR SIR:—It is with sincere regret that I cannot accept the kind invitation of your Committee to join with the people of your State and city in celebrating the memorable event, which had so much to do in shaping the destiny of our Western and Northwestern territory. Indiana will rejoice with her sister Michigan and extends her hand in cordial greeting.

The eleventh of July 1796, the lowering of the British flag to that of the young Republic, marked an important event, not alone in your State history, but in that of all states formed from that magnificent empire passing into the indisputable control of American freemen. It was indeed a vast empire opened up to a triumphant Christian civilization, and a race of strong, brave and resolute freemen. Your celebration will strike a responsive chord in every patriotic heart in Indiana, and we know the day will be fittingly and splendidly honored by your own brave and enterprising people.

Regretting my inability to be with you on behalf of the State of Indiana, I am, with high esteem,

Very truly yours,
CLAUDE MATTHEWS.

FROM SENATOR ALLISON.

DUBUQUE, IOWA, July 7th, 1896.

To the Honorable the Committee on Invitation of the One Hundredth Anniversary, Detroit, Mich.:

GENTLEMEN:—I have the honor to acknowledge receipt of your invitation to be present at the ceremonies commemorative of the evacuation of Detroit one hundred years ago. With thanks for your invitation, I regret that my engagements are such that I cannot have the pleasure to accept.

The event you commemorate, constitutes an epoch in the history of our country. It was the culminating act in completing our Independence. Though the Northwest Territory had been organized for some time, its settlement had been retarded by its continuous occupation by the British, which appeared to be indefinite until the Jay treaty fixed a time for the final departure of the British troops. This treaty, much abused when made, was of incalculable service not only to this region but to the whole country as well. It secured the rapid growth of the northwest and the creation of five populous states northwest of the Ohio and east of the Mississippi, and made necessary the acquisition of the territory west of that river, happily achieved through the Lousiana purchase only a few years later. Those who negotiated that treaty, and the one acquiring Lousiana, did not realize that within a century of time "The Northwest Territory," so called, and the contiguous territory lying west of the Mississippi, would embrace twelve great states, having an intelligent and cultivated population of twenty-three millions of people enjoying the blessings of free government, with an accumulated wealth of twenty-five thousand millions of dollars, or more than one thousand dollars for each inhabitant, and nearly two-fifths of the population and wealth of the whole country. Yet through the exertions of those who have come and gone within the century, and of those who still remain, these are the conditions existing at the end of the first century of the day you commemorate. May we venture the hope that those who commemorate the second century may be as prosperous and contented in the enjoyment of conditions equally favorable.

Again expressing my regrets, I am

Very truly yours,

W. B. ALLISON.

FROM SENATOR McMILLAN.

MANCHESTER, MASS., July 5, 1896.

MY DEAR SIR:—I regret that absence from the city will prevent me from joining my fellow citizens in the celebration of the one hundredth anniversary of the surrender of the post of Detroit to the United States, on July 11th.

With a foresight amounting almost to inspiration, our treaty commissioners insisted on drawing the boundary line so as to include Michigan within the territory of the United States, and when, for the purpose of retaining control over the fur trade, England refused to give up the Northwestern posts, the Jay treaty finally gave us possession of the territory George Rogers Clark had so bravely won by the sword; and nine years later civil government according to American ideals was set up within our borders.

It is fitting that these anniversaries should be observed, in order that the eventful history of nearly two centuries may teach us to prize the inheritance perfected for us by three great nations.

I am, Very truly yours,

JAMES McMILLAN.

Hon. Don M. Dickinson, Chairman Committee on Invitations, Detroit, Mich.

A WORD IN EXPLANATION.

The foregoing pages form the official report of the committee on publication of Evacuation Day Exercises. The following pages include those articles of an historical nature that appeared in the Detroit papers at the time of the celebration.

While I have had no hand in writing any of the articles, I have thought them worthy of preservation, and have collected and reprinted them solely with that object in view.

Many of the papers were prepared from data derived from books and unpublished manuscripts in my library; but the hasty manner in which the articles were originally written did not permit such thorough investigation as should precede such work and many errors are apparent. These I have not felt at liberty to correct and they are here reproduced as they first appeared.

The copies of Canadian Archives, the Askin Papers, the Cadillac Correspondence, the Montreal Manuscripts, the Orderly Books of General Wayne, consulted by the writers and referred to in these pages, are in manuscript in my library.

C. M. BURTON.

ANTHONY WAYNE.

(From the Detroit Journal, July 11, 1896.)

"Mad Anthony Wayne!" It is a name, indeed, to conjure with, one that brings to mind the stirring deeds and stern hardships of those early pioneers who made possible not only our beautiful City of the Straits, but the great commonwealths whose fertile acres are the most fitting monuments to the men who made the "middle west."

Among all those whose bravery or sagacity helped to win peace and bring prosperity to this section, no name is held in higher esteem than his, and no one man combined in a higher degree these attributes. There are men who actually mold events, and others who make the operation possible by their work as forerunners, and Wayne's connection with the western country was of the latter nature. For too long a period, Wayne has been looked upon simply as the most dashing officer of the Continental army, a man who knew not fear, and was as rash as he was brave. History sometimes lingers in giving a man his rightful due, but at length the time has come when we honor Gen. Wayne, not alone for his matchless daring, but for his wise counsel, unselfish patriotism and wise administration of whatever trust was given to him.

Anthony Wayne was born at Waynesborough, Pa., on January 1, 1745. His family was of English stock, but had been settled in America for three generations at the time of the Revolutionary outbreak. At school he was considered incorrigible, because of his fondness for military matters, which led him to spend more time in building miniature fortifications and drilling his schoolmates than in learning his lessons. He became a surveyor, and at the outbreak of the Revolution was a farmer at Waynesborough. At this time he was a man of considerable importance in the community. Early in 1775 he had raised a regiment, of which he was appointed colonel, and from that time he belonged to his country.

Through all the stormy time that attended the birth of our republic, no sword flashed brighter than Wayne's. He was made brigadier-general in the early part of 1777, and placed in command of the Pennsylvania troops. Under his stern discipline and gallant leadership they became renowned as the very pick of the Continental army.

No more dashing exploit is recorded of any leader than the storming of Stony Point, on July 15, 1779, where, in a skillfully planned assault, Wayne was shot down, but insisted on being raised and carried into the fortress at the head of his troops.

One of the characteristic, though unauthenticated stories of Wayne, is that when Washington asked him if he would storm Stony Point, he replied: "General, I'll storm h—l if you will plan it." The truth is that Wayne was a skillful soldier and his opinion was always sought by Washington upon strategic moves.

Through all the varied and shifting scenes of the Revolution, Wayne shone resplendent, and his service extended from Canada to Georgia. And when our independence had been finally acknowledged by England and her troops left our eastern shore, Wayne sheathed his sword and retired to private life, hoping to enjoy the repose he had won and so well deserved.

He had an honorable position in his native state, and served her in civil life with wisdom and zeal. Removing to Georgia, he was elected to congress, but only served about six months.

His quiet was again broken, for the Indians on our western border were becoming more and more troublesome, and in 1792 Washington called Wayne from his retirement and appointed him commander-in-chief of our army. Henceforth his career is linked with the west, and his military and diplomatic skill was never more severely tested than in his conflict with the wily savages, who were supported and urged on by British agents.

At the time of Wayne's accession to the command of the army, our interests in the northwest were in serious jeopardy. The lands beyond the Ohio had been settled by emigrants from all parts of the country, including very many old soldiers. The Shawnee and Miami Indians, under able leadership, determined that the encroachment of the whites upon their territory should stop at the Ohio, and for years they waged a bitter and merciless warfare upon our exposed frontier. Efforts had been made in 1790, under Gen. Harmar, and in 1791 under Gen. St. Clair, to crush the power of the Indian confederacy, which had its center in northwestern Ohio, near the lake, and within easy reach of Detroit, where the British had a strong outpost. Both these expeditions had resulted in disaster, and not only was the army demoralized, but these defeats increased the terror among the settlers, and depredations became more frequent. Fifteen hundred men, women and children had paid the penalty of frontier life with their lives, between 1783 and 1790, and the nation seemed powerless to protect our settlements.

"MAD ANTHONY" WAYNE.

The army of Harmar had been a collection of ill-armed, undisciplined men, led by officers, who, though brave, did not understand border warfare, while St. Clair's defeat was due simply to his lack of caution.

But with Wayne's accession new spirit and courage were infused. The army was reorganized upon a plan which permitted cohesion, and ease in handling, and Wayne's stern discipline and high reputation as a soldier soon brought order out of chaos.

Arriving in Pittsburg in June, 1792, he set about his arduous task. Many of the trusted officers who had served under him in the Revolution had been sacrificed to the incompetence of Harmar and St. Clair, while the terrors of the late campaigns made recruiting very slow. Wayne labored patiently, and the effect of constant drill and efficient officering soon began to show itself in the increased confidence of the men. He wintered his command at a point on the Ohio river, 27 miles below Pittsburg, and early in 1793 located a camp at Fort Washington, upon the site of Cincinnati. Although the sentiment of the country in general was averse to an Indian war, he did not relax his vigilance, and his little army became every day more efficient and better disciplined.

Wayne's letters at this time indicate great familiarity with the situation and a perfect understanding of the people he was to defend, and of the foes he was to subdue. When at last all negotiations failed, he advanced to a position 80 miles north of Cincinnati, which he called Greenville, and there passed the winter of 1793-94.

International complications were threatened with England, and Wayne was authorized to reduce the English post at the rapids of the Miami if he deemed it necessary.

Full discretionary power to lead in this most delicate position, was given by the government to the man whom we are accustomed to hear of only as "Mad Anthony" Wayne, and he handled the matter with the firmness of the soldier and the skill of the diplomat.

During the winter he had established a fort on St. Clair's battlefield, which he named Fort Recovery. This fort was attacked about the first of July, 1794, but the Indians were repulsed. Wayne now felt that it was time to act, and moved forward to the junction of the Glaize and Miami rivers, where he built Fort Defiance. Making another overture for peace, which was spurned, he met the Indians on August 20, 1794, at the rapids of the Miami, and inflicted upon them a defeat which brought peace forever to this section of the country, so far as the Indians themselves were concerned. The power of the Indian confederacy was broken, and Wayne's victory opened the way for the vast flood of immigration, which has transformed the wilderness of a hundred years ago into one of the garden spots of the world.

Insignificant so far as the number of men engaged, a mere skirmish compared to the battles of our late war, it was yet one of the decisive battles of our history. In addition to settling for all time our claim to the territory in dispute, it had a most important effect upon the negotiations then in progress at London, which ended in Jay's treaty. Up to this time, the English ministry had persisted in holding the English posts within our borders, but upon news of the battle reaching London, an agreement was soon reached, which resulted in the evacuation of these posts, one of the chief of which was Detroit.

After a visit to Pennsylvania, which was cut short by threatened war with England, Wayne returned to the border, empowered to act as the agent of the government in conducting negotiations for the delivery of the posts which had been ceded to us. His appointment to this mission was in effect a notice that there would be no trifling or delay while he had charge of the matter. And there was none. The posts were Niagara, Oswego, the Miami and Detroit, and in the beginning of June he was ordered to visit these posts and take possession of them in the name of the United States. Invested by his commission with civil as well as military powers, he executed his double mission with faithfulness and discretion.

After visiting the different posts, he at last arrived at Detroit, in September, 1796. During his progress nothing had occurred to hinder the success of his mission, and he had been received in every case in a courteous and friendly manner. At Detroit he found many Indians, who could hardly express admiration enough, for he was one of the truly brave who are recognized and admired, even by savages.

The transfer of Fort Lernoult, which then stood upon the site of the present city, took some time, and Wayne remained here until the middle of November. The material composing the rank and file of our army was not of the best in those days, and Wayne's rule was stern, but he looked after his men's welfare, and his sternness and harsh discipline were needed to control his turbulent followers.

Leaving Detroit about the middle of November, he sailed for Presqu' Ile, the site of the present city of Erie, Pa. When nearly there, he was seized with an attack of gout, which had tormented him for years. He was taken to the quarters of the commandant and lingered there in agony for several weeks, dying on December 15, 1796. By his own wish, he was buried on a high hill near the block house, and overlooking the shining expanse of Lake Erie. His remains were removed by his son in 1809, and taken to Pennsylvania. The site of the grave was lost for a time, but finally discovered, and in 1879 a monument was placed over it.

No man more than Wayne—called "Mad Anthony" by his soldiers in love for his fearless daring, but really a man of consummate skill and judgment—contributed to the foundation of the glory and prosperity of the great states that surround Lake Erie. By one stroke he broke the power that threatened all our border, and opened our fertile plains to the immigrants. And right well has his labor been repaid. For as long as men love brave deeds and brave leaders, so long shall be heard in our land the name of "Mad Anthony Wayne."

OUR CENSUS IN 1782.
(Detroit Journal, July 11, 1896.)

An earlier census of Detroit may have been taken, but the first of which we have any record is to be found in the Canadian archives for 1782. It is entitled: "A survey of the settlement of Detroit, made by the order of Maj. De Peyster, 16th day of July, 1782." The major estimated that in addition to those found by the enumerators in and around the fort, there were 100 in the king's service who were on detached duty out among the Indians "in the country." Adding these, the total population was 2,291, as follows:

Heads of families	321
Married women	254

Widows and hired women	72
Young and hired men	336
Boys	526
Male slaves	78
Girls	503
Female slaves	101
Total	2,191

De Peyster didn't go into the "survey" as extensively as modern superintendents of census, but he probably enumerated everything in sight. Moreover, it didn't take him a decade to compile the returns, but on the 20th he forwarded his completed survey to the governor-general at Quebec.

The remainder of the report is as follows:

Horses	1,112
Oxen	413
Cows	837
Heifers and steers	452
Sheep	447
Hogs	1,370
Flour, pounds	29,250
Wheat, bushels	1,804
Indian corn, bushels	355
Wheat sown last fall, bushels	4,075
Arpents under corn	521
Arpents under oats	1,840
Arpents under cultivation	13,770
Supposed bushels potatoes in the ground	3,000
Barrels cider supposed will be made	1,000

EARLY SHIP-MAKING.

(Detroit Journal, July 11, 1896.)

His majesty, George III., did one good thing for Detroit. If he was not the original ship-builder here, he put his money into the industry and fostered it. More than 100 years ago he had a fleet of sailing craft on the lakes to transport his soldiers, ordnance and stores between Newark, Bois Blanc, Detroit and Michilimackinac, and they bore away his armies when Jay's treaties went into effect.

Shipcarpenters' wages were not exorbitant in those days, when Askin's blotter is taken into consideration. The first report on this industry is entitled: "Muster roll of officers, carpenters, blacksmiths, employed in his majesty's shipyard at Detroit, from 29th December, 1777, to 24th April, 1778, both days included."

Richard Cornwall, master builder, received 10 shillings sterling per day, and John Shipley, storekeeper and clerk of the check, 100 pounds sterling per year. All the other employes were paid in New York currency, and at the following rates: Foreman of the yard, 12 shillings per day; assistant foremen, 8 shillings per day, and some of them 10 and 8 pounds per month; carpenters, 4 to 8 shillings, and one received 12 pounds per month; sawyers, 4 to 8 shillings per day; blacksmiths, the same, and the foreman 9 pounds per month; laborers, 4 pounds per month.

EVACUATION DAY.

(From the Detroit Tribune, July 11, 1896.)

It is not exact to say that the people of the United States were made independent by the war of the Revolution, or that their independence was completed with the evacuation of Detroit by the British forces, just a century ago today. Their independence was really a fact from the moment the cavaliers set sail for Virginia and the Pilgrim Fathers for New England. The war of the Revolution was, strictly speaking, only an effective assertion of what already was and had been for nearly two centuries.

The independence of the people of the United States is a habit of mind. It is not a mere political dissent. It is not comprised in having thrown off British government. The throwing off of British government was but one among countless manifestations of our independence. Our ancestors of those times did not so much make themselves free as they proclaimed to the world the freedom that they already had. It was a notification to all nations of the fact that the United States of America were able to go it alone.

The evacuation of Detroit was important politically; it was still more important as the symbol of great things. We are to celebrate today a very notable expression of national character. The spirit of independence which forced the British to leave our soil forever is still alive. It burns with undiminished brightness. We have never ceased to be independent. We have always proceeded without misgivings as to our separate destiny. Firm has ever been our faith in our mission to lead, and with the grace of heaven firm it always will be.

Forecaster Conger, of the weather bureau, last night predicted fine weather for the Evacuation day celebration today. It is expected that the celebration will draw to the city a large number of visitors. All the railroads and steamboat lines entering the city will run cheap excursions from all points. The hotels and restaurants have made extra preparations to care for the multitude.

Everything is in readiness for the celebration, which will begin promptly at 10:30 o'clock, except for the crowds to arrive. The decorations on the inside of the new postoffice are all completed. The chairs have all been put in position. The memorial tablet has been put in place on the west side of the Fort street entrance, and will be unveiled the first thing after the exercises begin.

Yesterday noon the executive committee held a meeting and inspected the new government building. They expressed entire satisfaction with the preparations at the building, and extended a vote of thanks to Chairman Harry F. Chipman, who had the details in charge.

THE EVACUATION.

(From the Detroit Tribune, July 11, 1896.)

It was Monday, July 11, 1796, and the scene was the British military post of Detroit. The sun rose brightly over the little town, and Fort Lernoult, and the broad expanse of the beautiful river. At the first notes of the bugle that sounded forth the reveille the Union Jack—the meteor flag of England—was given to the breeze, the main gate or entrance to the fort was opened, and red-coated sentinels were seen on guard. The few privates left in the fort fell into ranks and answered to their names, and then dispersed to get their breakfasts and help pack up.

There was to be no guard-mounting that day.

All around could be seen wagons loaded with household goods, and military supplies, for the "flitting" had commenced several days before, and the work of building Fort Malden, at Amherstburg, had been going on for several weeks.

On the ramparts several officers conversed in groups, apparently on a subject of engrossing interest, and the massive form of Col. Richard England appeared on the scene. Telescopes were brought out and the river below was scanned with interest.

Everybody in Detroit knew that, by the terms of the Jay treaty, the fort and its dependencies were surrendered by England to the United States, and t. at possession was to be given on July 1. But from several causes the United States troops had not come to claim their own. ... the intervening days some evil disposed soldiers or others had destroyed several of the windmills that lay on the river bank, and did some other mischievous acts, but these were not probably sanctioned by the commandant, who was a gentleman and an old and experienced soldier.

THE YANKEES CAME.

It was about 10 o'clock when the telescope discovered two vessels coming around the bend of the river below the town. The flags were not at first distinguishable, but in a short time they became plainer to the lookers, and the word went round:

"The Yankees are coming!"

Nearer and nearer came the two vessels, which were small schooners, each flying the Stars and Stripes. At this time a number of officers and men went down to the King's wharf, which then projected about 150 feet into the river at the foot of Shelby street. At the wharf were several loaded vessels, all ready to clear. The American vessels tacked in and were fastened to the wharf, around which were gathered a motley group of Indians, soldiers and white settlers.

There is no record of how the small American advance force was received. It was strictly on a peace footing, for it numbered only 65 men. The two vessels also contained several cannon, ammunition and provisions, the whole being under the command of Capt. Moses Porter. Being officers and gentlemen, it is more than probable that Col. England and his subordinates received them at the wharf with courtesy and good feeling. That the latter feeling predominated is certainly true, for the records show that the British commissary at Chatham loaned 50 pounds of pork to the United States commissary for the use of the troops.

Meanwhile the only one to show emotion was the renegade, Simon Girty, the miscreant who had laughed when Crawford, the American officer, was being burned at the stake by the Indians near Sandusky. He seemed anxious to leave what was now American territory, and too impatient to wait for the ferry boat, he spurred his horse into the river and swam it over to Canada. On the bank on the opposite side he stopped and furiously cursed the American government and its soldiers. Like Marmion, when he had got outside of the Douglas castle,

> His shout of loud defiance pours
> And shook his gauntlet at the towers.

And then came the ceremony of taking possession. The 65 United States troops formed and marched up the hill to the fort. They were probably received by the few British troops that were left with military honors. The British flag came down at noon, and then the starry banner of the free was hoisted, and Detroit and the northwest became United States territory.

A letter written by Col. England a few days later on Bois Blanc island, at the mouth of the Detroit River, shows that he was in Detroit at the time of the evacuation.

There was certainly no reason why he should not be present at that time. The two nations were at peace, and the evacuation was the result of an amicable treaty, and it would have been boorish and discourteous for him to be absent.

On the 13th came Col. John Francis Hamtramck, who was in command of this post until the arrival of his superior officer, "Mad Anthony" Wayne, who came in September.

A GREAT EVENT.

(From the Detroit Tribune, July 11, 1896.)

In this centenary celebration of Evacuation day is commemorated one of the most important events in early American history. Yet the final abandonment by the British of the lake frontier and the great northwest—a domain far more extensive than the original 13 colonies which so gallantly vindicated their claim to freedom and independence— was attended by no sensational feature. In the occurrence itself there is little to inspire the writer to eloquent periods reciting the number of the slain, the stirring episodes of conflict, the brilliancy of diplomatic intervention, or the profundity of statesmanship, through which the course of national destiny is determined. It was a cut and dried affair, with rather prosaic details.

It was like the quiet meeting of Grant and Lee at Appomattox, which was only a settling up of a military result, and lacked the coloring of pomp and pageantry, which was accompanied by nothing dramatic, save by association. Yet in the brief interview of these two great military representatives there was solved forever the problem of human liberty in the United States, and the perpetuity of a government by one people was assured.

So the evacuation of Detroit a hundred years ago was far less imposing than its commemoration of today, but it was a climax of long years of struggle with arms and diplomacy, and its outcome was of deep historical significance. The evacuation was but a link in the chain.

Still, it is surprising that there is so little of record concerning the leaving of Detroit by the British and its occupancy by the American government. Some of the enterprising merchants doing business here at the time were wont to make entries of interesting local events in their account books, but in none of these that have been perused by Detroit's antiquarians can be found any direct reference to the evacuation.

As further showing the paucity of information regarding the actual deliverance of the fort there is cited the fact that the only original map of Detroit in 1796 is now in the archives of the minister of marine in Paris. This work was done by Gen. Collot, who acted as a spy in this region at the behest of his government, and it shows the fortifications and surroundings of the British fort in this city. The map itself, of which there is a fac-simile in the office of C. M. Burton, and a reproduction in Farmer's History of Detroit, is a convincing proof that the French still entertained hopes of reoccupying this region when a favorable period presented itself.

ENGLAND AN IRISHMAN.

(From the Detroit Tribune, July 11, 1896.)

Several years ago the private letters of Col. Richard England, the last English commandant of the post, were given to the world. It was naturally supposed that his letters, written after the time he was here, would contain information concerning the incidents attending the evacuation. He was a good soldier and a cultured gentleman, as his writings amply attest. But the papers contain nothing but the kindliest references to those he left behind, and a few details of business he was anxious to close. This might have been a matter of delicacy on the part of the colonel, because his friends here were under a new regime, or it might have been because he was absorbed in new duties which demanded his attention. A prima facie proof that he was a brave fighter is the fact that he was born in County Clare, Ireland, and took to the profession of arms from choice. When he returned to England the Prince of Wales, afterward George IV., noticed his immense size and distinguished bearing—he was six and a half feet in height—and asked a friend who he was.

"It is Col. England," was the reply.

"England!" said the prince. "He ought to be called Great Britain."

In after years the colonel settled in Upper Canada and was interested in a colonizing company which placed settlers on lands in the extreme western part of that province. It is worthy of note that in 1793, while in command here, a son was born who bore his father's name. He also followed his father's footsteps, entered the British army, and for distinguished services was promoted step by step until he became lieutenant-general, and in time was knighted. Sir Richard England died in 1883, aged 90 years.

FORT LERNOULT.

(From the Detroit Tribune, July 11, 1896.)

Even as to Fort Lernoult, which was built by the English in 1778 and evacuated in 1796, there is a conflict of testimony. For instance, Col. Daniel Brodhead, then in command at Pittsburg, wrote Gen. Washington under date of November 22, 1779:

"The Delaware chiefs inform me that the new fort at Detroit is finished, and that the walls are so high that the tops of the barracks can scarcely be seen from the outside, but they don't know whether there are any bombproofs, as they are not permitted to go into the fort. They think the number of soldiers there does not exceed 300, and some part of that number remains in the old fort."

After studying the authorities at his command, Historian Silas Farmer describes the fort as made by piling up butts of trees with sharpened ends projecting outwards to a height of four feet. On top of this foundation and extending outward at an angle of 45 degrees, were heavy, sharpened stakes, and surrounding all was an earth embankment 11 feet high. The top of the parapet was 12 feet broad and the width of the ramparts at their base was 26 feet. Surrounding the embankment was a ditch 6 feet deep and 12 feet wide at the top, having in it a row of pickets 11 or 12 feet high. It was 40 feet from the fort to the banks of the Savoyard River, which was reached by a precipitous descent. This description would seem to negative the account of the Indians, as told by Brodhead.

Others who have written about the matter, or who speak from tradition, are inclined to the belief that the fort was not a very formidable affair even for those times. The circumstances under which it was erected, however, favor the idea that it was calculated to withstand a vigorous siege by a much larger force than that defending it. News had reached Detroit that the American general, Brodhead, was advancing from the southeast with a superior force in 1778, having already reached a position on what is now northern Ohio, which he was fortifying, his ultimate purpose being to make his way to Detroit and capture this important point on the frontier. The old stockade and block houses were considered by the British to be inadequate in the event of such an emergency. It was Maj. Lernoult that approved the plans for better defenses, Capt. Bird superintended their construction, and it was named after the major. The facts that Brodhead did not make the expected advance, and that Gen. Clark, commanding the American forces, did not make good his threat to occupy the fort as soon as it was completed by the British, does not lessen the probability that it was capable of making a stubborn defense. There were some difficulties in engineering that were not overcome entirely, such as the constant filling in of the ditches and the caving of the ramparts and glacis, which were caused by the water of the springs in the enclosures, but the work of strengthening and enlarging was generally continued by the garrison until the treaty of peace was signed between the two countries.

WHAT A CHANGE.

(From the Detroit Tribune, July 11, 1896.)

Some idea of the great improvements which have taken place within 100 years can be gathered from the fact that the fort occupied what is now the site of the government building, its centre being about the present intersection of Fort and Shelby streets. Its northern bastion extended nearly to Lafayette avenue; the western bastion extending nearly to Wayne street, the southern extending to the alley behind St. Paul's church, on the corner of Congress and Shelby streets, and the eastern extending to the Peninsular bank building on Fort street.

The town of Detroit, two-thirds of which was in the stockade, lay east and south of the fort. The citadel was near what is now the northwest corner of Jefferson avenue and Wayne street. The powder magazine was a little east of the intersection of Congress and Wayne streets, and was half way between the citadel and the fort. The three points were connected by a subterranean passage. The stockade, composed mostly of cedar posts, 14 feet in height, with its strong gates and block houses, were regarded by the British as a sufficient reliance against an attack by Indians, but the threatened attack of the Americans called for the erection of a fort. The entrance of the fort was on the southern side, through an archway of trees, and a drawbridge over the ditch.

THE KEY OF THE NORTHWEST.

(From the Detroit Tribune, July 11, 1896.)

The importance of Detroit itself at that time lay in the fact that it was a military point which was the key to the great northwest. It was also the depot of the fur trade and Indian supplies on the entire frontier. Although founded by Cadillac in 1701, it had not grown much in the 95 years following, and was a village of only about 300 houses and 2,600 inhabitants, which included about 200 male and female slaves. Its streets, laid out in the French style, were narrow, the broadest, which occupied the present line of Jefferson avenue, between Griswold and Wayne streets, being only 30 feet wide. The houses and stores were entirely built of logs and were very small, space being economized to the utmost within the stockade. The chief source of income to the merchants was in supplying the troops and Indians, and dealing in the furs abundantly supplied by the Indians, trappers and organized companies. Surrounding the little town was a dense, primeval forest, pierced by no roads leading into the interior, save by Indian trails. The Detroit River and the lakes were the thoroughfares of travel, so far as there were any, and all the points of beauty now surrounding the city were obscured by a monotonous, trackless wilderness, relieved only by the noble river which was then, and is now, the crowning grandeur of the City of the Straits. The most frequent visitors were Indians, who came here for various purposes. Under British rule some were soldiers, others came here to dispose of their peltries, and others to loaf and get drunk on rum, which was then the cheapest spirituous liquor in those parts. The British supplied rum to the Indian troops as part of the commissary supplies, but under American rule there were efforts made to withhold intoxicants from the red men. Generally, however, they found a way to gratify their cravings for strong drink. Open scenes of drunkenness in the town of Detroit under British rule were always witnessed after the Indians returned from successful forays against American settlers. On such occasions the red men, flushed with victory and rum, would dash through the narrow streets, waving poles, on which bloody scalps were fastened, and yelling like fiends, while the inhabitants would prudently fasten their doors. The savages, however, seldom attacked the inhabitants, and most of their difficulties were between themselves. The presence of the soldiers was a bar against any attacks on the settlers or merchants. Sixteen years after the evacuation, when the British captured Detroit, the Indians had the American residents at their mercy, and committed many depredations.

A more extended description of Detroit, in 1796, is given by a traveler named Isaac Weld, and appears on another page.

OUR OLD RESIDENTS.
(From the Detroit Tribune, July 11, 1896.)

Of the character of her people Detroit has always had just cause to be proud. In the early days, besides the French pioneers who sought homes and lands in the new territory, there were men of means and education who came to this point because it offered profitable business inducements in the fur and Indian trade. Some of these men, like James May and the Macombs and Abbotts, conducted business on a large scale, and have an enviable place in history because of services rendered this country when Great Britain sought to retain this portion of its territory. Some of the ancestors of the oldest and best families in Detroit laid the foundations of their wealth in this city, which has been increased to large fortunes in later years by good management and business ability, but principally by the enhancement of land values which always follows the increase of population.

Notwithstanding their isolation from civilized centers, and the martial and aboriginal environment of the place, these men provided religious and educational facilities for their families, and enjoyed social pleasures under what would seem to be most forbidding circumstances. There were boat races, athletic sports, dancing, parties, picnics, equine contests and social functions which are customary at the present day. All the old correspondence which has been preserved shows that the leading men of Detroit in those bygone days were of a superior class, and their old-fashioned, punctilious courtesy was exceedingly charming and refined, but too elaborate for the rush and push of modern days. These combined attractions, with the potent addition of their cultivated and beautiful wives and daughters, made Detroit a favorite frontier post for the military who, of course, were favored guests at the best houses. The limited communication with the outer world only served to bring the members of the little community into closer intimacy.

WHY ENGLAND DELAYED.

The above is a brief and perhaps imperfect description of the social, military and commercial situation of Detroit in 1796. Why this section was not evacuated by the British 13 years before, in compliance with the treaty of 1783, has ever since been a subject of controversy, and has not yet been determined. It was among the stipulations of that treaty that Great Britain should be allowed a reasonable time within which to withdraw her forces from this country, but even the most radical defenders of the British policy do not attempt to claim that her action was justified under this provision. It would be the acme of absurdity to hold, after taking years to defeat an invading enemy, that he should be allowed twice as many years to withdraw from this country. The contention made by the British and their defenders ever since has been that the United States had failed to comply with the requirements of the treaty. A special count in this charge was that British merchants were creditors of merchants in this country; that the new government had agreed in the treaty to guarantee the payment of these debts; that several states had refused to comply with this agreement because they had no constitu-

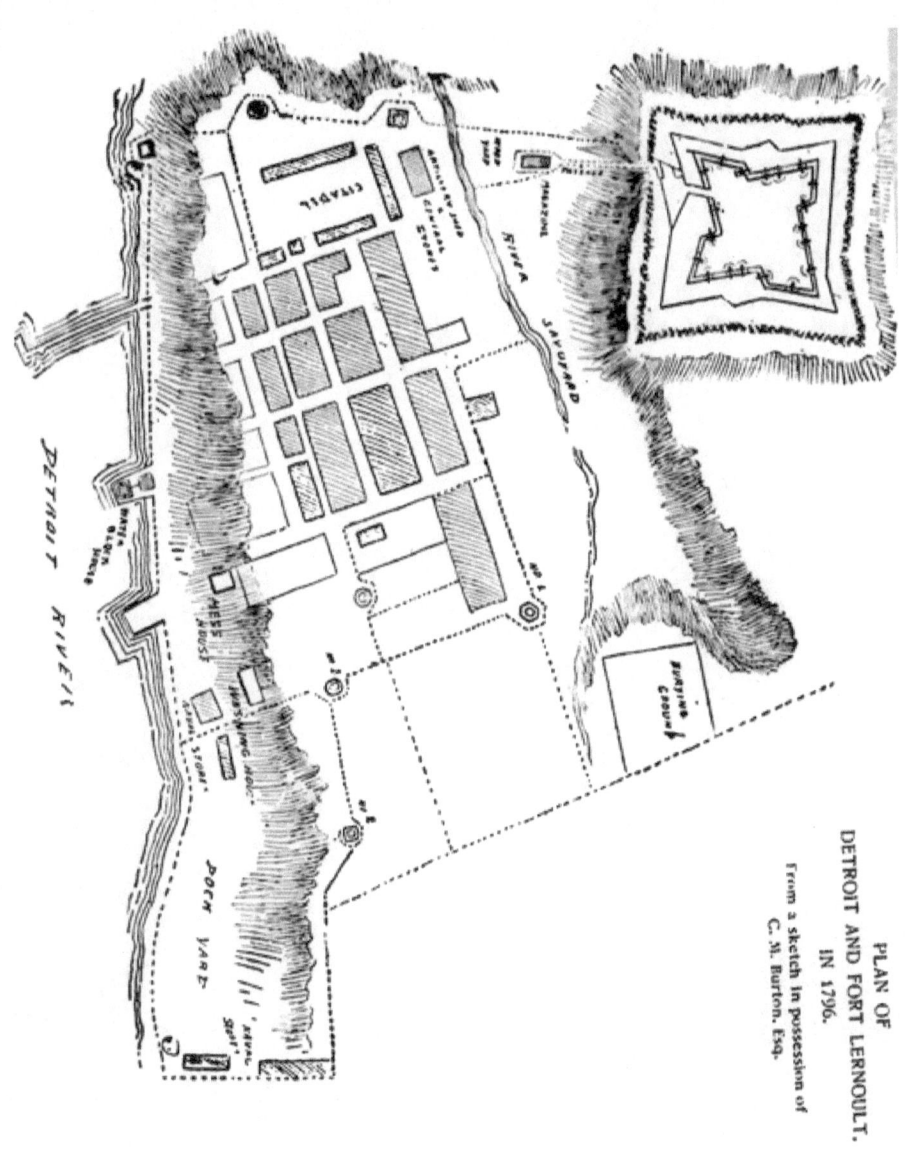

PLAN OF
DETROIT AND FORT LERNOULT,
IN 1796.
From a sketch in possession of
C. M. Burton, Esq.

tional right to do so; and because of all this the British government rightly refused to surrender the sovereignty of the northwest territory until the British merchants were paid or secured. This engendered a bitterness which not only led to a sharp diplomatic correspondence, but in 1794 made a second war imminent.

ENGLAND'S ULTERIOR MOTIVES.

The generally accepted theory among American authorities is that the excuses made by the British for not carrying out their treaty agreements were merely pretexts to cover their determined purpose to retain possession of the northwest. The reasons for this purpose were apparent. It gave the control of the lucrative fur trade, which was a virtual monopoly in the hands of the Hudson Bay Company and the merchants of Montreal. The representatives of these interests in London were in close touch with the British government, which is always solicitous for the advancement of trade—a nation's chief strength. The retention of the northwest would also give a vantage ground from which to renew the war against the colonies. The English never give up a project until after they are defeated, and sometimes not then, and there was a strong sentiment at home that this territory should be reclaimed by the mother country. Above all things it would enable the British to retain the support of the Indians, who could be depended on to fight England's battles in the event of war. That this object was not only entertained, but that it succeeded, is evidenced by the fact that the Indians of the west, in the American territory, were the allies of the British in the war of 1812.

In this struggle England's savage contingent committed some of the most devilish atrocities in the annals of so-called civilized warfare.

AN ATROCIOUS POLICY.

There is also damning evidence that the English incited the Indians against the American white settlers, and were responsible for the most horrible crimes against men, women and children. It is shown by official records that as far back as 1791 the redskins were being urged to violence by the infamous Simon Girty and other agents, and that under Girty's orders they assisted in bringing guns to Detroit for the purpose of strengthening the British position. In 1793, prompted by the same power behind the throne, the general council of Indians declared that they would not believe that the United States intended to do them justice unless it was agreed that Ohio should be the boundary line between the Indian territory of the northwest. This was in accordance with the British policy of having a "buffer state" next to their own dominions in America, which could be controlled in the British interests. The American government would not acquiesce in this proposition to alienate the northwest, because it knew that it was inspired by Great Britain.

In 1794 Lieut.-Col. England was in correspondence with Lieut.-Gov. Simcoe, of Canada, in regard to the Indian troubles. Simcoe had sent several letters to the Indian head men, and his statements in these letters were repeated at Montreal and were communicated to the United States government. The letters clearly indicated that, whether with or without authority from the home government, British officials were secretly urging the Indians to continue their warfare against the Americans, and promising that aid and comfort would be furnished the former. This led to a diplomatic correspondence between the two countries. Simcoe denied that he had been intriguing in this matter, and asked to be investigated. An investigation was held in Montreal, but it was conducted in such a manner that it simply covered up any offenses of which he might have been guilty.

WAYNE'S INDIAN CAMPAIGN.

About this time Indian Agent McKee, of the British forces, notified Lieut.-Col. England that the Delawares had taken the scalps of six American infantry at a point between Forts Washington and Hamilton, and that these scalps were to be forwarded to the lake Indians for the purpose of inciting them against the United States troops. Nothing was done to prevent or discourage this scheme, and it had the sanction and guilty knowledge of the British officials. This was of special significance, because Gen. Anthony Wayne was then about advancing to the northwest, and the Indians were being rallied to oppose him.

Gen. Wayne fortified the Glaize and planned to proceed thence toward Detroit, despite any opposition which might be encountered as the result of Indian plans or those of the English. He offered $1,000 reward for the scalp of Simon Girty, the cruel but capable renegade. These facts gave the frontier posts an excuse for strengthening their position on the pretext that they feared an intent on the part of Wayne to invade Canada. They had further apology for this course because one Christopher Miller, whose character was not above suspicion, made oath before British officials that he, at the request of Wayne, had told the Indians that it was not against them, but against the English, that he and his forces were moving, and that he intended to drive the British from the country.

EASILY CONVINCED.

Upon this scant and unreliable evidence the English officers were content to act. Simcoe pushed the construction of gunboats on the Thames as rapidly as possible, and urged the prompt enlistment of additional seamen as well as land forces.

Near Fort Miamis, on the Maumee, in the vicinity of where Toledo now stands, Wayne whipped the Indians, who had concentrated to meet him, in August, 1794. The English commandant at the fort made complaint both to his superior officer and to Wayne, because the latter had fought within range of the guns of Fort Miamis. What the English chose to term the pretentious reply of "Mad Anthony" was thoroughly characteristic of the man. He practically informed the complainants that he knew his business and would attend to it. This precipitated a hot correspondence between Wayne and Campbell, the latter being in command at the fort. He served notice on the American general that he must not again get within gunshot of the fort or he would be fired upon.

STRAINED RELATIONS.

These facts and incidents go to show the strained relations existing and how easily another war with Britain might have been brought about. In the meantime our government was doing everything possible to bring about by peaceful means, a compliance with the treaty of 1783. Not only were diplomatic means employed through representatives in England, but direct communication was had with Gen. Haldimand, Gen. Campbell and other commandants, requesting that they evacuate, or in the event of failure to comply at once that they specify the time within which they would yield undisputed possession to the territory held under their adverse control. These officials temporized until they could receive authoritative orders, and they were invariably to the effect that the posts be held. Everything went to show that Great Britain meant if possible to retain her grip.

PEACE AT LAST.

It was while affairs between the two powers were in this critical condition that John Jay, the distinguished American jurist and statesman, was sent to negotiate the second treaty of peace made necessary by the policy of non-compliance persisted in by the English. This minister plenipotentiary was especially well equipped for the delicate task. He had been president of congress, was the first chief justice of the supreme court of the United States, and served as governor of New York. As the result of his official negotiations with Great Britain, she receded from all her adverse claims in this country and agreed to evacuate all the posts then retained by June 1, 1796. There was a disposition in some quarters to criticise the Jay treaty, but it is the testimony of Lord St. Helens that Jay was not only chiefly but wholly the means by which it was brought to a successful conclusion. It was under the provisions of this treaty that Col. Hamtramck first took charge of Fort Miamis and a few days afterwards assumed command at Detroit.

JOHN FRANCIS HAMTRAMCK.

No name of that time is better known in Detroit than that of Hamtramck, and a brief review of his record shows that he was born in Canada in 1757, and died in this city in 1803. He commenced his distinguished service in the Revolutionary war as captain of Dubois' New York regiment, and before he died was commissioned a colonel. He especially distinguished himself as commander of Wayne's left wing in the battle with the Indians near Fort Miamis, as above described. He was not only a great soldier, but a man of marked ability in other directions. His officers held him in the highest esteem and erected a monument to his memory on the grounds of St. Anne's church. When the burial ground was discontinued his remains were removed, and now lie in the Elliott lot in Mt. Elliott cemetery.

Two years after taking command here Col. Hamtramck had a son, who also distinguished himself. When but 16 years old he was with Zachary Taylor's expedition up the Mississippi. They had a severe engagement with the Indians and British off the mouth of Rock River, Ill. The lad showed his fighting blood in a way to excite general admiration, and the reward was a gratification of his desire to enter West Point. He served with distinction throughout the Mexican war and afterwards became a planter in Virginia.

So far as the lives of those who comprised the people of Detroit was concerned, the evacuation made but little difference, although the change gave an impetus to the growth of its business as well as of its population. Though Gen. St. Clair was appointed governor, he never came here, and Winthrop Sargent acted in that capacity. Wayne county was organized, and had dimensions to warm the cockles in the heart of the latter day politician. It included all the present state of Michigan, the eastern half of Wisconsin, and large portions of Indiana, Illinois, and Ohio. This modest county took in what is now Chicago, Toledo and Cleveland as far east as the Cuyahoga River.

THE WALK IN THE WATER.
From an Engraving in Possession of C. M. Burton.

THE BOIS BLANC DISPUTE.

There came upon the village the shadow of another war when Lieut.-Gov. Simcoe began to fortify Bois Blanc island under the claim that there was an intent on the part of the Americans to take possession of it. On the protest of this government he was commanded to desist, and the question of ownership abided the negotiations which followed. Under the treaty that had been ratified, the boundary line between the American and British possessions in this country was to follow the line of the deepest channels of the waters dividing the two countries. This prevented all dispute until Bois Blanc was reached on the route from the east. Here there was a long controversy, for a strict construction of the treaty would have given the island to America and left the Canadians a comparatively narrow strip of water at that point. Gen. Cass insisted that the island belonged to this country, and so urged upon Henry Clay, then secretary of state. But the latter appears to have been moved by a strained sense of equity and made the concession. For this he was severely censured in congress and by the country at large.

DEFEATED LAND GRABS.

In 1795, while the two nations were quarreling about the sovereignty of the northwest, and when the clearheaded British citizens were beginning to realize that the territory would inevitably pass under the dominion of the United States, several big land grabs were planned by citizens of Detroit, who were British sympathizers. These grabs seemed to have been conceived with a view to acquiring the lands by private ownership after the British sovereignty over them had ceased. One of them was conceived in the mind of a Dr. Robert Randall, and it contemplated the securing to private ownership 20,000,000 acres of land, comprising the entire lower peninsula of Michigan, with parts of Ohio, Indiana and Illinois. The plot was far reaching, for Randall had interested in the northwest such men as John Askin, John Askin, Jr., Robert Innes, William Robertson, David Robertson and Jonathan Scheiffelin. There were also partners manipulating the scheme at Philadelphia, then the seat of government. Some distinguished men of New England were also involved, and members of congress were on the ground floor. Their petition offered the government $500,000 for the land.

OFFERED AN INDUCEMENT.

An additional inducement held out to the government for the confirmation of the titles was the claim that the Indians within the territory ceded would be kept quiet by its owners. Just how they expected to control the savages does not appear in the developments made, but this proffer was in keeping with the rest of the swindling operation. Congressmen were to be bribed with stock and promoters were to be generously cared for.

But the enterprise was destined to failure. On December 28, 1795, Hon. William Smith, member of congress from Virginia, arose and calmly exposed the whole conspiracy, stating openly that an attempt had been made to bribe him by Randall. Murray, of Maryland, and Giles, of Virginia, announced that like infamous proposals had been made to them, as did James Madison and others. Randall and Whitney, of Vermont, were placed under arrest and held for nearly a month while congress had the matter under discussion. There were also civil arrests made at the request of President Washington. But there were so many men of influence implicated that the investigations were whitewash affairs, and the conspirators escaped with the ignominy they had brought upon themselves.

About the same time John Askin and his associates had conceived several other colossal land grabbing schemes. The territory on the south shore of Lake Erie, between the mouth of the Cuyahoga River and Sandusky, a distance of 59 miles, and running back an equal distance, making a tract of about 2,400,000 acres, was held by the Indians. By promises of rum, guns, money, etc., 34 chiefs were induced to affix their totems to a deed conveying the tract to this syndicate. Askin also engaged in a similar transaction by which he acquired an Indian title to a large tract on the Maumee River. For pressing these claims John Askin, Jr., was arrested at Greenville by the American authorities, and was in jail a short time. Of course the claims were not allowed by the government, and the deeds are valuable only as historical curiosities.

A TRAVELER'S DESCRIPTION.

Isaac Weld made a tour of the states and Canada in 1795-6, and in 1799 published a book, as most travelers did in that day. He visited Detroit in October, 1796, three months after the evacuation of the town by the British, and his description of the town is of interest at this time, the centennial of the American possession.

"Detroit contains about 300 houses," he wrote, "and is the largest town in the western country. It stands contiguous to the river, on the top of the banks, which are here about 20 feet high. At the bottom of them there are very extensive wharfs for the accommodation of the shipping, built of wood, similar to those in the Atlantic seaports. The town consists of several streets that run parallel to the river, which are intersected by others at right angles. They are all very narrow, and not being paved, dirty in the extreme whenever it happens to rain; for the accommodation of passengers, however, there are footways in most of them, formed of square logs, laid traversely close to each other.

"The town is surrounded by a strong stockade, through which there are four gates, two of them open to the wharfs, and the two others to the north and south side of the town respectively. The gates are defended by strong blockhouses, and on the west side of the town is a small fort in form of a square, with bastions at the angles. At each of the corners of this fort is planted a small field piece, and these constitute the whole of the ordnance at present in the place. The British kept a considerable train of artillery here, but the place was never capable of holding out for any length of time against a regular force; the fortifications, indeed, were constructed chiefly as a defense against the Indians.

"Detroit is at present the headquarters of the western army of the states; the garrison consists of 300 men, who are quartered in barracks. Very little attention is paid by the officers to the minutia of discipline, so that however well the men may have acquitted themselves in the field, they make but a poor appearance on parade.

"The belles of the town are quite *au desespoir* at the late departure of the British troops, though the American officers tell them they have no reason to be so, as they will find them much more sensible and agreeable men than the British officers when they know them, a style of conversation, which, strange as it may appear to us, is yet not at all uncommon amongst them. Three months, however, have not altered the first opinion of the ladies.

"I cannot better give you an idea of the unpolished, coarse, discordant manners of the generality of the officers of the western army of the states than by telling you that they cannot agree sufficiently amongst themselves to form a regimental mess; repeated attempts have been made since their arrival at Detroit to establish one, but their frequent quarrels would never suffer it to remain permanent. A duelist and an officer of the western army were nearly synonymous terms, at one time, in the United States, owing to the very great number of duels that took place amongst them when cantoned at Greenville.

THE TOWN'S INHABITANTS.

"About two-thirds of the inhabitants of Detroit are of French extraction, and the greater part of the inhabitants of the settlements on the river, both above and below the town, are of the same description. The former are mostly engaged in trade, and they all appear to be much on an equality. Detroit is a place of very considerable trade; there are no less than 12 trading vessels, belonging to it, brigs, sloops and schooners, of from 50 to 100 tons burden each. The inland navigation in this quarter is indeed very extensive, Lake Erie, 300 miles in length, being open to vessels belonging to the port, on the one side, and Lakes Michigan and Huron, the first upwards of 200 miles in length and 50 in breadth, and the second no less than 1,000 miles in circumference, on the opposite side; not to speak of Lake St. Clair and Detroit River, which connect these former lakes together, or of the many large rivers which fall into them. The stores and shops in the town are well furnished, and you may buy fine cloth, linen, etc., and every article of wearing apparel, as good in their kind, and nearly on as reasonable terms, as you can purchase them at New York or Philadelphia.

SHORTAGE OF SALT.

"The inhabitants are well supplied with provisions of every description; the fish in particular, caught in the river and neighboring lakes, are of a very superior quality. The fish held in most estimation is a sort of large trout, called the Michilimackinac whitefish, from its being caught mostly in the straits of that name. The inhabitants of Detroit and the neighboring country, however, though they have provisions in plenty, are frequently much distressed for one very necessary concomitant, namely, salt. Until within a short time past they had no salt but what was brought from Europe; but salt springs have been discovered in various parts of the country, from which they are now beginning to manufacture that article for themselves. The best and most profitable of the springs are retained in the hands of the government, and the profits arising from the sale of the salt are to be paid into the treasury of the province. Throughout the western country they procure their salt from springs, some of which throw up sufficient water to yield several hundred bushels in the course of one week.

DAUGHTERS FOR SALE.

"There is a large Roman Catholic church in the town of Detroit, and another on the opposite side called the Huron church, from its having been devoted to the use of the Huron Indians. The streets of Detroit are generally crowded with Indians of one tribe or another, and amongst them you see numberless old squaws leading about their daughters, ever ready to dispose of them, pro tempore, to the highest bidder. At night all the Indians, except such as get admittance into private houses, and remain there quietly, are turned out of town, and the gates shut upon them.

"The American officers here have endeavored to their utmost to impress upon the minds of the Indians an idea of their own superiority over the British; but as they are very tardy in giving these people any presents, they do not pay much attention to their words. Gen. Wayne, from continually promising them presents, but at the same time always postponing the delivery when they come to ask for them, has significantly been nicknamed by them Gen. Wabang, that is Gen. Tomorrow. * * *

"The country round Detroit is uncommonly flat, and in none of the rivers is there a fall sufficient to turn even a grist mill. The current of the Detroit River itself is stronger than that of any of them, and a floating mill was once invented by a Frenchman, which was chained in the middle of the river, where it was thought the stream would be sufficiently swift to turn the waterwheel; the building of it was attended by considerable expense to the inhabitants, but after it was finished it by no means answered their expectations. They grind their corn at present by windmills, which I do not remember to have seen in any other part of North America."

THE FIRST FAMILIES OF DETROIT.

(From the Detroit Journal, July 11, 1896.)

Detroit is remarkably fortunate in the number of its old families which are still flourishing and prominent in the business interests of the city. Many of these are sprung from the most influential families of the old world, and one, at least, the Navarre, is sprung from a race of kings. This name appears no more in Detroit records, for the reason that it is represented only upon the mother's side. The founders of several of these families are known to have come with Cadillac; and the founder of one, in fact, is fabled to have been here already and to have been one of the Indian traders who met Cadillac on the banks of the Detroit. All have been equally prominent in the affairs of our home, and from the earliest times their members have appeared on the side of whatever was most for the interest of their community.

To one family especially we are indebted for brave acts, and here and there a life lost in war with Indians; to another for many of our first buildings. Each family displays some characteristic which marks it in every generation. To all we are indebted for the same loyalty and energy. As time has passed, younger generations of these same families have carried on the work of their fathers, and have maintained the same standing in public affairs. For today, as 150 years ago, many of the same names are prominent and influential.

DETROIT IN 1820.

A Sketch by Gen. Alexander Macomb. In possession of C. M. Burton, Esq.

One family, as has been said above, is claimed to have been here before Cadillac in 1701. A few were founded in the first ten years after his arrival, five or six in the period of reviving prosperity after the depression of 1715; but the greatest number came to the city between this time and 1760. From this time on to the end of the century, the period of activity, this score of families, bound together by marriage and friendship and the common object of securing the best results for our city in every difficulty, were the leading factors in the control and the history of the town.

Living in a small stockade, and bound by the ties of a common danger and common amusements, these families, representing the influential and aristocratic part of the colony, intermarried to such an extent that there is scarcely one of the original names which has not, as a part of it, several of the others. By reason of this intermarrying and the lack of male heirs, nearly half of the original names no longer appear in public records.

Another reason that one recognizes today so few of the old French names is that as the town came under English and American influence the French names were frequently translated. Still another reason is the great number of names a Frenchman had, and his inconsistency in using them. For instance, the founder of Detroit, whose name in full was "Antoine de la Mothe Cadillac," usually signed himself "Lamothe Cadillac," but often he is found in records as "Antoine Lamothe," "La Mothe" or "La Motte."

But the most important reason is that the old inhabitants, living so much in common with the Indians, and consequently acquiring many of their customs, gave names to each other, describing some well known trait in their character, or some incident in their life, and these nicknames often superseded the true ones.

Although there are few definite records to be found as to the early grants, it is probable that as each bona fide settler came to Detroit he received from the commandant a grant of four arpents, nearly equal to three and a half of our acres. The order of their establishment is as a general fact shown in the position of their farms, the oldest families holding those nearest the heart of the present city, or, as it was then, nearest the stockade. Nearly all of these farms bordered on the river and the original positions of many of them is preserved in the manner of the streets running through them at right angles to the river.

Owing to neglect in the arranging of other details, Cadillac was not vested with the power to make grants when he founded the city. In fact, he did not receive the legal right before 1705, though farms were allotted to the settlers long before that. The conditions of some of these king's grants were curious enough. In one, made by Cadillac in 1707, the grantee, or one who received the farm, was bound to pay rent of about $3 a year to the king. He was bound to begin clearing his land before three months from the time he received it. All timber such as could be used for fortifications or vessels was reserved for the government. The privilege of hunting rabbits, partridges and all small game was reserved to the grantor, Cadillac. The grantee was bound to help raise on the first day of May of each year a long Maypole before the door of the principal manor house. All the grain was ground at the manor mill and a fixed price was paid for grinding. A tax was to be collected for the king on every transfer of the land, and before a sale the tenant must give the authorities notice, so that should the government be willing to pay the price offered by the would-be purchaser, it should have the option of buying. The grantee was absolutely forbidden to sell or trade intoxicating liquors to the Indians. He was bound to make his fences in a specified manner, and, if called upon, to help in the construction of his neighbor's, and he was also bound to permit such roads upon his land as were deemed necessary for the public good.

By the terms of this grant, it is quite evident that the government intended the commandant to be master.

THE CAMPAU HOUSE ON JEFFERSON AVENUE.

One has only to be an observer to learn how well the Campau family preserves its prestige. It was founded in Detroit in 1707 and 1708 by Michel and Jacques. The family still hold the greater part of their original grant, and in the rapid growth of the city it has become exceedingly valuable and was, a few years ago, one of the two most valuable estates.

The Godfroy family is sprung from a race that was in the 17th century, second only to royalty. One of their ancestors was secretary of state and syndic of the French republic. The founder in Detroit was Pierre Godefroy, as it was then spelled, who came in 1715. He and his immediate descendants had heavy interests in the Canadian fur trade. Pierre's line died out and the real founder was Jacques, who came shortly after his kinsman. His son Jacques figured prominently in the Pontiac war. After his attempted treachery, Pontiac tried to regain the confidence of the commander, Maj. Gladwin, by asking for a conference. The officer, while granting the request for a parley, relaxed none of his vigilance. He sent Jacques Godfroy and Jean Chapoton. Nothing being accomplished, the chief threw off his mask of friendliness and made an open attack upon the fort.

This family has so intermarried with the other pioneer families that the greater number of its members living now are enrolled under other families.

Alexander Chapoton, Jr., is the best known of the representatives of this family living here. The family was founded before 1720 by Jean, the second physician of Fort Pontchartrain. For 40 years he held this commission for the French government, and retiring a few years before the surrender to the English, settled on his grant. That he held the interests of the settlement dearest to his heart is evident in the fact that he gave to the colony 20 children. One of these, Jean Baptiste, was the companion of Jacques Godefroy at his unsuccessful parley with Pontiac.

The founder of the Navarre family was distantly related to Henry IV., the line being unbroken from the Duke de Vendome, Henry's father. Robert Navarre came to Detroit in the office of royal notary some time before 1734, at which time he is known to have married. The branch is still preserved through the mother's side in many of our most prominent families today.

Zacharie Chiquot was the founder in 1736 of the Cicotte— as it is now spelled—family. This family was famous in the early days for the fine collection of silver plate in its possession. Remnants of this fine property are still owned by the descendants.

About a large family whose early members were hardy and adventurous, there necessarily hang many traditions, part truth and part imagination. Told from generation to generation as they have been, and interwoven with the weird superstitions of the red men and pioneers, these stories have reached us as pure legends. It is related of Jean, son of the founder Zacharie, that, at one time, when by royal edict, liquor had been forbidden to be sold or traded to the Indians, and they, in consequence, had threatened to sell their fine winter's gathering of furs to the English, he was sent secretly by De Tonty, the commandant, with the purpose of intoxicating the natives and then buying their furs. His errand was successful, but as he was returning to the fort he was set upon by goblins and the Loup-Garou, the devil in the form of a wolf, and his ill-gotten load taken from him. This family is no longer represented under the same name in Detroit.

The Barthe family is represented still in Detroit by Mrs. Richard Storrs Willis, though the name itself was lost by marriage two generations ago. Founded some time before 1747 in the last of the same century, it was large and flourishing.

The Dubois family was founded in several branches at different times before 1750. Though well known up to the last generation, the representatives now in Detroit are few.

The Baby family, though in its early generation closely connected with our city's history, has in the last half of a century rather died out in Detroit, the greater number living in Canada, where it is still represented in the first ranks of every vocation. Its founder in Detroit was Jacques Duperon Baby, who arrived before 1760. His name figures prominently in the siege of Pontiac.

The Moran family are now, as they were when the founder of the name, Charles Morand Grimard, was first mentioned in Ste. Anne's records, in 1706, active and influential. The family is scattered throughout Canada. Before the division among his sons, at the death of Judge Charles Moran, the estate left was the third largest in Detroit.

One branch of the Moran family was distinctly related to the wife of Cadillac. It is told how, long ago, Jacques Morand, as the name was spelled then, met and loved the daughter of an Indian trader who pitched his camp with the Indians on the shore of Lake St. Clair. But the maiden was already consecrated to her God. She had long wished to enter a convent, and the wish had just been granted. This only served to madden her lover, who, at the price of his soul, assumed the form of the Loup-Garou, the phantom wolf. In this form he persuaded the pious girl, who saved herself by a prayer which turned the monster to stone.

These nine are the families still most influential in our city, but there were many others, including the Beaufait, Chene, Beaubien, De Quindre, Desnoyers, Gamelin, Marantay, Rivard and St. Aubin, which were in the early days influential and public-spirited, but which have either died out or married under new names in the last few generations.

EARLY DETROIT.
(From the Detroit Journal, July 11, 1896.)

Sheldon's "Early History of Michigan" says that Fort Pontchartrain, built by Cadillac in 1701, was about the size of the city square, and occupied the ground from Jefferson avenue to Woodbridge street, which was then the water's edge, and from the Cooper block on the east (T. A. McGraw & Co.), to a little west of the old Michigan Exchange, now Pingree & Smith's.

At the time of Pontiac's conspiracy, in 1763, the fortifications had been greatly extended, and the entire town was within the palisades. This inclosure extended from where now is Griswold street to the westerly line of the old fort; from the river to where now is the alley between Jefferson avenue and Larned street, the inclosed space being about 1,200 yards in circumference. The east entrance was called Pontiac's gate, after the conspiracy. Ste. Anne street was about at the south line of Jefferson avenue and Ste. Anne's church stood on the north side. On the south side there was a large military garden, in which stood a block house. Here the officers met for consultation, and here the Indian councils were held. The church and the block house were the only public buildings in the town.

When the Americans marched into the inclosure 100 years ago, the eastern boundary had been extended up the line of Griswold street across the Savoyard creek to about the north line of Congress street, and there ran off westwardly to the southeastern angle of Fort Lernoult, or Shelby, as it was thereafter called, this angle being south of Fort street and east of Shelby. The western boundary was at Cass street, and crooked eastwardly to intersect the western angle of the fort, giving the town a somewhat triangular form.

The first settlers were French, and they had intermarried with the Indians. During British dominion here a few English and Scotch families came in and took up grants of land along the river. By 1796 all these had become prosperous. They owned large numbers of cattle, horses and sheep, and raised all the grain their necessities required. This was ground in the old French windmills, one being near the mouth of the Savoyard, and a second one at the Rouge. The women did not know how to spin or weave, and the fleeces from the sheep were used to cover cellar windows, and for other like purposes.

The vexatious cartwheel plan that has the Campus Martius and Grand Circus for its hubs, was the work of Judge Woodward, who gave his name to the axle. September 8, 1806, he submitted a bill for the incorporation of Detroit as a city. It was passed on the 13th and entitled "An act concerning the city of Detroit." Two days later the first bank of Detroit was incorporated, but congress revoked its charter in 1809. The bank building was on the northwest corner of Jefferson avenue and Randolph street, and the directors paid $395.75 for the lot.

In laying out the new city, Ste. Anne street was widened and became Jefferson avenue. The site of Ste. Anne's church was in the middle of it. Fr. Gabriel Richard, vicar-general of the order of Sulpitians, asked the governor and judges to allot a new site, and a site for an academy for boys. At the same time Angelique Campau and Elizabeth Williams, nuns, sent in a petition for a lot upon which to erect an academy for girls. For these purposes the land on the south side of East and West avenue (Cadillac square), between Bates and Randolph streets, to Larned street, was given. In 1807 the Protestants asked for a lot upon which to build a church, and the northeast corner of Woodward avenue and Larned street was given.

In 1806 the second Indian conspiracy for the destruction of Detroit was hatched. Tecumseh and his brother, Ellshwatawa (the Prophet), encouraged by the British, sowed disaffection amongst the Wyandots and other tribes near Detroit, and in 1807 matters became so threatening that the governor ordered the inhabited portion of the new city to be inclosed with a strong stockade. The eastern boundary of this stockade was at Brush street, and the western was near Cass street. There was a gate at Brush and Atwater streets, and a block-house just east of the Biddle House. The western gate was on Jefferson avenue, about 100 feet west of Cass street. About the time the palisade was completed

Hull effected a treaty with the Ottawas, Chippewas, Pottawattomies and Wyandots; Tecumseh and his Shawanese were left alone, and the conspiracy was at an end.

CAPTIVE WHITE BOY STOLEN BY INDIANS IN OHIO AND BROUGHT TO MICHIGAN.

(From the Detroit Journal, July 11, 1896.)

In 1793, O. M. Spencer, then a lad of 12, in after years a minister of the gospel, while at play with other boys near Cincinnati, was taken captive by a prowling band of Miami Indians and brought to their village near the present site of Fort Wayne. His parents sought the assistance of Gen. Washington, and at his request Gen. Simcoe, commander-in-chief of the British forces in the northwest, directed Col. England, then in command at Detroit, to ransom the lad. This was done, but a few months elapsed before he could be sent to Cincinnati, and during this time he remained with the colonel at Fort Lernoult.

Even at that age young Spencer was an intelligent and observing lad, and kept a daily journal of all he saw and heard. Subsequently this journal was published, and the following is the boy's description of Detroit three years before it became an American possession:

"Detroit is a small town, contains only wooden buildings, but few of which are well furnished, surrounded by high pickets inclosing an area of probably half a mile square, about one-third of which, along the bank of the river, as the strait is called, is covered with houses. There are four narrow streets running parallel with the river, and intersected by four or five more at right angles. At each end of the second street is an entrance, secured by heavy wooden gates. North of this street, at the west end of the town, is a space about 200 feet square, inclosed on a part of two sides with palisades, within which a row of handsome two-story barracks, for the accommodation of the officers, occupies the west side, and buildings of the same height for the soldiers' quarters stand on the north and a part of the east side. The open space is a parade ground, where the troops are every day exercised by the adjutant.

"In the northwest corner of the large area, inclosed with pickets, on ground slightly elevated, stands the fort. It is separated from the houses by an esplanade, and is surrounded, first by an abatis of treetops about four feet high, having the butts of the limbs sharpened and projecting outward; then by a deep ditch, in the center of which are high pickets; and then by a row of light palisades, seven or eight feet long, projecting horizontally from the glacis.

"The fort itself covers not more than half an acre of ground. It is square, with a bastion at each angle, and with parapets and ramparts so high as to entirely shelter the quarters within, which are bomb-proof. The entrance to the fort is on the south side, facing the river, and is over a drawbridge, and through a covered way, over which on each side are long iron cannon, carrying 24-pound shots, which the officers call the 'British lions.' On each of the other sides are two cannon, and on each bastion four, some six, some nine, and some twelve-pounders. By the side of the gate, near the end of the officers' barracks, there is a 24-pounder, and there are two small batteries of cannon on the bank of the river for the protection of the south side of the town.

"The fort is garrisoned by a company of artillery under the command of Capt. Spear, two companies of infantry, and one of grenadiers, of the Twenty-fourth regiment, which is Col. England's regiment. The other companies are at Michilimackinac and other northern posts.

"Anchored in the river in front of the town are three brigs of about 200 tons each. The Chippewa and Ottawa are new, and carry eight guns each. The Dunmore is an old vessel and carries six guns. There is a sloop, the Felicity, of about 100 tons, armed with two swivels. These vessels all belong to his majesty, George III., and are commanded by Commodore Grant. There are besides, several merchantmen, sloops and schooners, the property of private individuals."

After the Stars and Stripes began to wave above the fort, emigrants from France commenced to arrive and occasionally an American from the state would venture thus far into the wilderness. There were no sawmills, and lumber was cut by hand. The first Yankee trader to arrive was Stephen Mack. He erected a shanty and opened an emporium of fashion, selling calico at 75 cents, and "apron check" for $1 per yard. Tea cost $2 per pound.

On January 11, 1805, that part of the great northern territory lying between Lake Michigan on the west, Lakes Huron, St. Clair and Erie and their connecting rivers on the east, was organized into the territory of Michigan by an act of congress. William Hull was appointed governor; Augustus B. Woodward, Frederick Bates and John Griffin

VIEW OF DETROIT IN 1796.
From a Drawing in Possession of C. M. Burton.

judges, but they did not arrive until June 12. June 11, just five months after the territory was organized, a fire broke out at midday and at nightfall the village of Detroit consisted of one dwelling house on Ste. Anne street, a brick storehouse, and piles of smoking ashes. Hull and the other territorial officers were sworn in the second Tuesday of July, and then the people who had been living in tents and huts, became inspired with hope and courage, and commenced erecting houses. The fire had obliterated all lines and boundaries, but congress passed an act authorizing the governor and judges to lay out a new town, including all previous ground and 10,000 acres adjacent. Every person above the age of 17, who did not owe allegiance to a foreign power, and owned or occupied a house when the fire broke out, was given a lot of 5,000 square feet. What remained of the 10,000 acres was sold, and the proceeds applied to the erection of a courthouse and jail.

CONSPIRACY OF PONTIAC.
(From the Detroit Journal, July 11, 1896.)

The story of the conspiracy of Pontiac and other Indian chiefs to capture the fort in May, 1763, has frequently been written, but the following is the official report of Lieut. MacDonald to Lieut.-Col. Bouquet, under date of July 12 of that year:

"You certainly have heard long before now of our misfortunes at the Detroit and its dependencies, but as it may be satisfactory to you to be more particularly informed, do myself the pleasure to give you an exact account of all that has happened in this department, and hope that you'll do me the justice to believe that I would have written you and communicated the same long ago had an opportunity offered.

"On Friday, the 6th of May, we were privately informed of a conspiracy formed against us by the Indians, particularly the Ottawa Nation, who were to come to council with us the next day, and massacre every soul of us.

"On the morning of that day, being Saturday, the 7th day of May, 15 of their warriors came into the fort and seemed very inquisitive and anxious to know where all the English merchants' shops were. At 9 o'clock the garrison were ordered under arms, and the savages continued coming into the fort until 11 o'clock, diminishing their number as much as possible by dividing themselves at all the corners of the streets most adjacent to the shops. Before 12 o'clock they were 300 men, at least three times in number equal to that of the garrison, but seeing all the troops under arms, and finding the merchants' shops shut, I imagined prevented them from attempting to put their evil scheme in execution that day.

"Observing us thus prepared, their chiefs came in a very condemned like manner to council, where they spoke a great deal of nonsense to Maj. Gladwin and Capt. Campbell, protesting at the same time the greatest friendship imaginable to them, but expressing their surprise at seeing all the officers and men under arms.

"The major then told them that he had certain intelligence that some Indians were projecting mischief, and on that account he was determined to have the troops always under arms upon such occasions; that they, being the oldest nation, and the first to come to council, need not be astonished at that precaution, as he was resolved to do the same to all nations. At 2 o'clock they had done speaking, went off seemingly very discontented, and crossed the river half a league from the fort, where they all encamped.

"About 6 o'clock that afternoon six of their warriors returned and brought an old squaw prisoner, alleging that she had given us false information against them. The major declared she had never given any kind of advice. They then insisted upon naming the author of what he heard with regard to the Indians, which he declined to do, but told them it was one of themselves, whose name he promised never to reveal, whereupon they went off and carried the old woman with them. When they arrived at their camp, Pontiac, their greatest chief, seized on the prisoner and gave her three strokes with a stick on the head which laid her flat on the ground, and the whole nation assembled round her, and called repeatedly: 'Kill her! Kill her!'

"Sunday, the 8th, Pontiac and several others of their principal chiefs came into the fort at 5 o'clock in the afternoon and brought a pipe of peace with them, with which they wanted to convince us fully of their friendship and sincerity, but the major, judging that they only wanted to caggole us, would not go nigh them, nor give them any countenance, which obliged Capt. Campbell to go and speak to them, and after smoking with the pipe of peace, and assuring him of their fidelity, they said that the next morning all the nation would come to council, when everything would be settled to our satisfaction, after which they would immediately disperse, and that would remove all kind of suspicion. Accordingly, on Monday morning, the 9th, six of their warriors came into the fort at 6 o'clock, and upon seeing the garrison under arms, went off without being observed. About 10 o'clock o'clock we counted 56 canoes with about 7 and 8 men in each crossing the river from their camp, and when they arrived nigh the Fort, the gates were shut and the interpreter sent to tell them that not above 50 or 60 chiefs would be admitted into the Fort, upon which Pontiac immediately desired the interpreter in a peremptory manner to return directly and acquaint us that if all their people had not free access into the fort, none of them would enter it; that we might stay in our Fort, but he would keep the country, adding that he would order a party instantly to an island where we had 24 bullocks, which they immediately killed. Unluckily three soldiers were on the island and a poor man with his wife and four children, which they all murthered except two children, as also a poor woman and her two sons that lived about half a mile from the fort.

"After having thus put all the English without the fort to death, they ordered a Frenchman, who had seen the woman and her two sons killed and scalped, to come and inform us of it, and likewise of their having murdered Sir Robert Davers, Capt. Robertson and a boat's crew of six persons two days before near the entrance of Lake Huron, from which place they set off from here on Monday, the 2d, in order to know if these lakes and rivers were navigable for a schooner which lay here to proceed to Michilimackinac. We were then fully persuaded that the information given us was well founded, and a proper disposition was made for the defense of the fort, although our number was but small, not exceeding 120, including all the English traders, and the works very nigh a mile in circumference.

"On Tuesday, the 10th, early in the morning the savages began to fire on the fort and vessels which lay opposite to it. About 8 o'clock the Indians called a parley, ceased firing, and half an hour after the chiefs of the Wyandottes came into the fort on their way to council, where they were called by the Ottawas, and promised us to endeavor to solicit to and persuade the Ottawas from committing further hostilities After drinking glasses of rum they went off.

"At 3 o'clock, several of the inhabitants, and four chiefs, of the Ottawas, Wyandottes, Chippewas and Pottawattomies come and acquainted us that most of all the inhabitants were assembled at a Frenchman's house about a mile from the fort, where the savages proposed to hold a council, and desiring Capt. Campbell and another officer to go with them to that council, where they hoped with their presence and assistance further hostilities would cease, assuring us at the same time that be as it would, that Capt. Campbell and the other officers that went with him should return whenever they pleased. This promise was ascertained (asserted) by the French as well as the Indian chiefs, whereupon Capt. Campbell and Lieut. McDougall went off, escorted by a number of inhabitants and the four chiefs. The first promised to be answerable for their returning that night.

"When they arrived at the house above mentioned they found the French and Indians assembled, and after councilling a long time, the Wiandottes were prevailed upon to sing the war song, and this being done it was next resolved that Capt. Campbell and Lieut. McDougall should be detained prisoners, but would be indulged to lodge in a Frenchman's house till a French commandant arrived from Illinois; that next day five Indians and as many Canadians would be dispatched to acquaint the commanding officer at the Illinois that Detroit was in their possession, and required of him to send an officer to command, to whom Capt. Campbell and Lieut. McDougall should be delivered. As for Maj. Gladwin, he was summoned to give up the fort and two vessels, etc., the troops to ground their arms; that they would allow as many battoes and as much provisions as they judged requisite for us to go to Niagara; that if these proposals were not accepted of, they were 1,000 men and would storm the Fort at all events, and in that case every soul of us should be put to the torture.

"The major returned for answer that as soon as the two officers were permitted to come into the fort, he would, after consulting them, give a positive answer to their demands; but could do nothing without obtaining their opinion.

"On Wednesday, the 11th, several inhabitants came early in the morning into the fort, and advised us by way of friendship to make our escape aboard the vessels, assuring us we had no other method by which we could preserve our lives, as the Indians were then 1,500 fighting men and would be as many more in a few days, and that they were fully determined to attack us in an hour's time.

"We told the monsieurs we were ready to receive them, and that every officer and soldier in the fort would willingly perish in the defense of it rather than condescend or agree to any terms that savages would propose, upon which the French went off, as I suppose to communicate what he had said to their allies, and in a little afterwards the Indians gave their usual hoop, and about 500 or 600 began to attack the fort on all quarters. Indeed, some of them behaved extremely well, advanced very boldly in an open plain, exposed to all our fire, and came within 60 yards of the fort, but upon having three men killed and about a dozen wounded, they retired as briskly as they had advanced, and fired at 300 yards distance till 7 o'clock at night, when they sent a Frenchman into the fort with a letter for the major, desiring a cessation of arms that night, and proposing to let the troops with their arms go on board the vessels, but insisting on our giving up the fort, leaving the French artillery, all the merchandise and officers' effects, and had even the insolence to demand a negro boy belonging to a merchant, to be delivered to Pontiac.

"The major's reply to their extraordinary propositions was much the same as the first.

"Thursday, the 12th, five Frenchmen and as many Indians were sent off for the Illinois with letters wrote by a Canadian agreeable to Pondiac's desire. On the 13th, we were informed by the inhabitants that Mr. Chapman, a trader from Niagara, was taken prisoner by the Wiandotes with five battoes loaded with goods. The 21st, one of the vessels was ordered to sail for Niagara, but to remain till the June 6, at the mouth of the river in order to advert some battoes which we expected daily from Niagara. On the 22nd, we were told that Ensign Paullus, who commanded at Sandusky, was brought prisoner by 10 Ottawas, who reported that they had prevailed after a long consultation with the Wiandotes who lived at Sandusky, to declare war against us; that some days ago they came early of a morning to the blockhouse there and murdered every soul therein, consisting of 27 persons, traders included; that Messrs. Callender and Prenties, formerly captains in the

Pennsylvania regiment, were among that number, and that they had taken 100 horses loaded with Indian goods, which, with the plunder of the garrison was agreed on to be given to the Wiandotes before they condescended to join them; that all they wanted was the commanding officer.

"On the 29th of May we had the mortification to see eight of our battoes in possession of the enemy passing on the opposite shore with several soldiers aboard. Called at these in the battoe that if they passed the savages would kill them all, upon which they immediately seized upon two Indians and threw them overboard. Unluckily one of the Indians brought a soldier overboard with him and tomahawked him directly, they being near the shore and it quite shoal. Another soldier laid hold of an oar and struck that Indian upon the head of which wound he is since dead. Then there remained only three soldiers, of which two were wounded, and although 50 Indians were on the bank not 60 yards firing upon them the three soldiers escaped on board the vessel, with the Battoe loaded with eight barrels of provisions, and gives the following account of their misfortunes, viz.:

"That two nights before at 10 o'clock they arrived about six leagues from the mouth of the river, where they encamped; that two men went a little from the camp for firewood to boil the kettle, where one of the two was seized by an Indian, killed and scalped in an instant. The other soldier ran directly and alarmed the camp, upon which Lieut. Cuyler immediately ordered to give ammunition to the detachment, which consisted of one sergeant and 17 soldiers of the Royal Americans, three sergeants and 75 rank and file of the Queen's Independent Company of Rangers. After having delivered their ammunition and a disposition made of the men, the enemy came close to them without being observed behind a bank, and fired very smartly upon our flank which could not sustain the enemy's fire, and they retiring precipitately threw the whole in confusion. By that means the soldiers embarked aboard the Battoes with one, two and three oars in each Battoe, which gave an opportunity to the savages of taking them all except Lieut. Cuyler and 30 men that made their escape in the Battoes to Niagara.

"On the night of the 2nd inst. Capt. Campbell and Lieut. McDougall made a resolution to escape. It was agreed on between them that Mr. McDougall should set off first, which he did, and got safe into the fort. But you know it was much more dangerous for Capt. Campbell than for any other person, by reason that he could neither run nor see, and being sensible of that failing I am sure prevented him from attempting to escape.

"The 4th a detachment was ordered to destroy some breastworks and entrenchment the Indians had made a quarter of a mile from the fort, and about 20 Indians came to attack that party, which they engaged, but were drove off in an instant with the loss of one man killed and two wounded, which our people scalped and cut in pieces. Half an hour afterwards the savages carried the man they had lost before Capt. Campbell, stripped him naked, and directly murdered him in a cruel manner, which indeed gives me pain beyond expression, and I am sure cannot miss but to affect sensibly all his acquaintances. My present comfort is that if charity, innocence and integrity is a sufficient dispensation for all mankind, that entitles him for happiness in the world to come."

THE BLOODY RUN—TWO STORIES OF THE FAMOUS INDIAN MASSACRE.

It is an old and a trite saying that one story is good until another is told. The French and Indian account of the tragedies of July 4 differs very materially from the English story as told by Lieut. MacDonald. It is that Lieut. Hay and a number of soldiers started from the fort to the house of M. Baby, to get some powder and lead that had been left there. On the way they met the nephew of an Ojibway chief, killed him, tore off his scalp, and shook it toward the enemy. The chief ran to the house of M. Meloche, where Campbell was confined, bound him to a fence, shot him to death with arrows, cut off his head, tore out his heart and ate it.

The wanton killing of the Indian had fired anew the hearts of the chiefs, and it was determined to destroy the fort and all who were in it. Pontiac was at their head, a crafty and fearless leader, and he laid a plan of siege. The English inhabitants had fled within the picketed inclosure, and the Indians at once cut off all supplies from the outside. They knew, however, that relief would soon come from the forts below, and they resorted to every artifice and strategy known in savage warfare. To prevent the vessels anchored in the river from going after supplies, they attempted to destroy them with fire. They constructed a large raft up near the mouth of Parent's creek, piled it high with dry wood and brush, saturated the pile with tar, pushed the raft out into the stream, and when it had floated down nearly to the vessels applied the torch. The sailors at once slipped their anchors, and the vessels then floated as rapidly as the raft. Sails were run up and the vessels glided to a position of safety.

This was on the night of July 10, and as soon as the fire raft was in mid-stream the besieging host filled the air about the fort with blazing arrows. Some of them fell upon the houses and set them on fire, but a portion of the garrison extinguished the flames, while the remainder fired at every Indian who exposed himself. The attempt to destroy Detroit with fire was a failure, and Maj. Gladwin retaliated for the attempt by sending the vessel up and down the river to fire their cannon at the Indian villages and encampments.

Relief came to the besieged garrison on the 29th, when 22 barges came up the river bearing Capt. Dalzell, Maj. Rogers, 280 soldiers, cannon, ammunition and an abundance of stores. Indeed, the fort was too small to accommodate all the officers and men, and some of them were quartered at the houses of the inhabitants.

Dalzell had been a soldier in the east under Gen. Putnam, was a bold and fearless fighter, and held Indian warfare in contempt. He at once besought Gladwin to permit him to go out with a detachment and drive the savages away, but Gladwin knew the danger of going into the forest to fight with natives of the forest, and though he at first refused, finally yielded. At 2 o'clock in the morning of July 31 Dalzell, at the head of 250 men, left the fort and marched as silently as possible up the river road, two large bateaux, each carrying a swivel and a number of artillerymen, moving up the river to support him.

Pontiac, however, had in some manner gained intelligence of the projected movement, and early the previous evening had summoned his chiefs and their warriors to a council at a large tree that then stood on the banks of Parent's Creek, just below where Jefferson avenue now crosses its buried channel, and there they waited the attack. This was ever after called "Pontiac's council tree," and old residents well remember it. It was cut down a few years ago, but its stump is still pointed out to visitors. The tree has frequently been called "Pontiac's Oak," and "Pontiac's Elm," but it was a whitewood.

It was a starlight night, and as the close columns of Dalzell's command neared the banks of the creek the ambushed Indians, themselves invisible, poured in a deadly fire. The troops returned the fire, but they might as well have saved their bullets. Dalzell attempted to drive the savages from cover by charging, but they slipped from tree to tree and remained invisible. Their fire was incessant and gallant, and Capt. Grant, who commanded one detachment, ordered a retreat. Capt. Rogers, in command of the other wing, fell back to the house of Jacques Campeau, which stood on the river bank between the present Dubois and Chene streets, and there maintained his position.

Dalzell saw that nothing but loss was to be gained by fighting with a hidden foe, and directed his command to fall back beyond the range of their bullets. He endeavored to carry back a wounded soldier, and was himself shot dead. By this time each detachment was surrounded by maddened Indians, but maintained their positions until daylight, when reinforcements arrived from the fort, and at 8 o'clock the defeated troops reached their quarters. Eighteen had been killed, three taken prisoners, and 38 wounded. The Indians mutilated the body of Capt. Dalzell and left it where he fell. It was brought to the fort by a son of Jacques Campeau, and buried in the "King's Garden," within the fort. Parent's Creek was ever after called "Bloody Run."

In 1772 Jacques Campeau sent the following petition "To the King's Most Excellent Majesty":

"In the year 1763, when the different nations of savages had attacked the fort of Detroit, commanded by Col. Gladwell (Gladwin), and your majesty's troops there had sallied out against them, but being few in number were constrained to retreat, your petitioner very cordially received 250 of them into his house, who were unable to reach the fort, and from whence they fought against the savages some time, when your petitioner, his wife and family, administered to them all the comfort his dwelling could afford, nevertheless and notwithstanding your majesty's orders to the contrary, your petitioner's house was plundered of effects to the value of $300; that after that disaster had subsided your petitioner applied to Col. Gladwell for a pecuniary recompense for the injury he had suffered in his property, who most equitably ordered a court martial to inquire into the amount of your petitioner's losses, which upon a fair inquiry, they reported at $300, as by the papers remaining in your majesty's archives at Detroit, fully appears, but your petitioner, notwithstanding such inquiry and report has not been paid any part of it, but still remains altogether unindemnified."

JOHN FRANCIS HAMTRAMCK.
(From the Detroit Journal, July 11, 1896.)

When his distinguished rank and military services are considered, and especially the fact that after fighting in the war of the Revolution to aid the colonies to win their independence, and that, this accomplished, the remaining 20 years of his life were given to the northwest, fighting Indians with Gen. Wayne until the departure of the British from the line of forts stretching from Erie to the Straits of Mackinac, compelled them to leave the warpath and sue for peace, and then taking command of the fortifications here, making a home here on the banks of the river, remarkably little is known of the private life of John Francis Hamtramck.

Appleton's Encyclopaedia says he was born in Canada in 1757, but does not give the date nor the place. As a youth it takes him over into the state of New York, and makes him a soldier in Dubois' regiment.

The late Robert E. Roberts, in his little history of Detroit, published in 1863, says that Hamtramck was one of the gallant French youths who came to this country with Gen. Lafayette, and served on his staff.

Roberts came here about 20 years after the death of Hamtramck, at a time when, and for years afterwards, there were scores of prominent citizens who had known the gallant officer personally, and beyond doubt he gained his information from them. Moreover, Roberts was a careful and accurate writer, who would not have spoken with positiveness had he been uncertain of his facts.

Both agree that Hamtramck served in the American army with distinction, and continued in the service as long as there was any fighting to be done for the struggling states. On the 29th of September, 1789, he was appointed a major of infantry. February 18, 1793, he was made a lieutenant-colonel and placed in command of the first sub-legion. He led the left wing of Wayne's army at the battle on the Miami, August 20, 1794, and was distinguished for his bravery.

He remained with Wayne's army, keeping the Indians in subjection by striking them heavily whenever they went on the warpath, and was placed in command of Fort Wayne October 22, 1794. When word was received in May, 1796, that the British were about to evacuate the posts they then held within the territory of the United States, Col. Hamtramck went down the Maumee to Camp Deposit and remained there until the 21st of June. A few days later the British surrendered Fort Miamis, and Hamtramck was there when he received orders to proceed to Detroit and take possession of Fort Lernoult.

Sacred
to the Memory of
John Francis Hamtramck Esq.,
Colonel of the U States Regiment of inf-ty,
and
Commandant of
Detroit and its Dependencies
He departed this life on the 11th of Ap' 1803
Aged 45 Years, 7 Months, & 28 days
True Patriotism,
And a zealous Attachment to rational Liberty
Joined to a laudable Ambition,
led him into Military Service at an early
period of his life,
He was a Soldier even before he was a man;
He was an active participator
in all the Dangers, Difficulties and Honors
of the Revolutionary War;
And his Heroism and uniform good conduct
procured him the Attentions & Personal Thanks of
the Immortal Washington.
The United States in him have lost
a Valuable Officer & a Good Citizen,
And Society an Useful & Pleasant Member;
to his Family the Loss is incalculable:
And his Friends will never forget
the memory of Hamtramck
this humble Monument is placed over
his Remains
by the Officers who had the Honor
to serve under his command.
A small, but grateful Tribute to
his Merit
and
his Worth.

INSCRIPTION ON HAMTRAMCK'S TOMB.

He had insufficient means for transportation, but July 7 two small vessels arrived from Detroit, and Hamtramck immediately hurried on board a detachment of infantry and artillery, 65 men in all, under the command of Capt. Moses Porter, a few cannon, ammunition and stores, and dispatched them with orders to take possession of Detroit and the fort and hold them until his arrival. Two days later he had procured a sloop of 50 tons, loaded it with flour, quartermasters' stores, ordnance and ammunition, and leaving Capt. Marschalk, Lieut. Shanklin and 52 infantry, a corporal and six artillery, in command of Fort Miamis, embarked on the sloop and 11 bateaux for Detroit, his troops numbering about 250.

Eight days later he wrote to Gen. Wilkinson from Detroit that the British evacuated on the 11th, and Capt. Porter took possession. Hamtramck and his command arrived on the 13th. "Mad Anthony" Wayne arrived about a month later, remained here until the middle of November, went to Presqu' Ile, now Erie, and died there December 14.

Col. Hamtramck remained at Fort Shelby, as it was now called, until April 11, 1803, the date of his death. His remains were interred in the burial ground adjoining Ste. Anne's church, in the square bounded by Larned, Congress, Bates and Randolph streets, and there reposed until about 30 years ago, when they were removed to Mt. Elliott.

(NOTE.—John Francis Hamtramck (or Hamtrenck) was a son of Charles David Hamtrenck and Marie Ann Bertin, and was born at Quebec August 16, 1756. His father, Charles David Hamtrenck dit L'Allemand was a barber and a son of David Hamtrenck and Adele Garnik of Luxembourg, diocese of Treves, Germany, and he married Marie Anne Bertin at Quebec, November 26, 1753.)—C. M. B.

The letter and record book of the colonel for the period he was stationed here is still in existence, but is a highly-prized possession of a family at Dayton, O. It was in the garrison when Hull made his cowardly surrender in 1812, and was taken away by an officer of Ohio militia among his personal effects.

ILE AUX COCHONS.

(From the Detroit Journal, July 11, 1896.)

Earliest Name of our Beautiful Park in Detroit River.

The possession of the Ile aux Cochons, now our own Belle Isle, was longer in dispute than Detroit. Cadillac granted it to the early settlers as a common, but nobody claimed any property rights in the island until about the year 1753.

Lieut. George McDougall, of his majesty's Sixtieth Regiment, had been a faithful officer, and about the year named was given a grant to the island by George III. and the council. He took possession, erected buildings, and cleared a portion of the land. Meantime two other residents of Detroit had applied to the crown for a grant of the island, but their applications had been rejected.

Ever since the grant of Cadillac the island had been common grazing ground, and after a time protest was made against the possession by McDougall. Sir Guy Carleton, writing to Lord Hillsborough from Quebec, July 8, 1769, says:

"The grants and papers have not yet been found among the public records here. It is a matter of doubt whether the right of common was ever given them by any formal instrument, but a fact well known, and ascertained by many persons of credit and reputation in the province, is that the Ile aux Cochons was granted about the year 1753, which grant was afterwards revoked upon the representations of the inhabitants of Detroit that this island was absolutely necessary for them to receive their cattle in summer to avoid the running wild in the woods, or the Indians destroying them in any of their drunken Frolicks.

"As it would appear the grant to Mr. McDougall was immediately from His Majesty, I thought it right to give your Lordship the earliest information of what has come to my knowledge about that matter."

The protest bears the names of many old French settlers, the descendants of whom are prominent in the Detroit of today, though in some instances the orthography has been slightly changed: Denoye, Miloche, Oulette, Lesperance, Langlois, Derouillard, Delisle, Dequindre, Labrosse, Chapoton. The Campeau family was represented by Jacques, Louis, Simmonet and Baptiste, pere and fils.

In the following May, McDougall wrote to the earl of Hillsborough: "By a paragraph of a letter from the Hon'ble Major.-Gen. Thomas Gage, commander in chief of his majesty's forces in North America, to the Hon'ble Major Thomas Bruce, of the 60th regt., commanding at this post, I understand that his excellency has given it as his opinion that the grant given me of Hogg Island by his majesty and council, referred to and confirmed by the express orders of the commander in chief in a letter to Captain Turnbull, then commanding at the fort, that I should, in consequence of an ill-supported claim made by some inhabitants of this place to said island as a common, give up my right and property to be decided by arbitration. I hope your lordship will be good enough to excuse me for declining to leave what I think my property, with the improvements thereto, agreeable to the tennor of my grant to such a decision.

"My lord, from your well known abilities to distribute strict justice to every subject within the limits of your administration, I have great reason to hope my past service and the justice of my cause, may in some degree entitle me to your lordship's protection."

McDougall sent with this letter a memorial, setting forth that the grant was coupled with the provisos that the transfer to McDougall must not give umbrage to the Indians, and that the improvements made by McDougall at the island be "applied to the more effectual and easy supply of His Majesty's fort and garrison at Detroit."

McDougall says he was aware that no absolute grant could be given, because Detroit was outside the boundary line laid down by his majesty and parliament in 1763, but he was contented to accept of an order of the council, judging it equally good as a real deed.

His majesty referred the matter to the commander-in-chief at Detroit, and told him to put McDougall in possession of the island or not, as he judged equitable. The commandant decided in favor of McDougall, and he entered into possession of the island.

To clear away the clouds upon his title, McDougall, on May 4, 1769, called the Indians together in council in the presence of all the officers of the garrison, "at which time he received a solemn deed for the said island, which cost him very considerably both in presents and provisions."

McDougall declares that when Col. Gladwin was in command, 1762-4, the inhabitants never pretended to have the least title or claim to the island, and it was Gladwin's "publick orders that no cattle should be put upon the island without his liberty, nor should anyone cut wood or hay on the island on any pretense whatever." This order was continued in force by Col. Campbell, who succeeded Gladwin.

Attached to the memorial was the following Indian deed, executed in the presence of witnesses at the council at the fort:

"This indenture made by and between Lieutenant George MacDougall, late of the 60 Regiment of the one part, and Oketckewandng, Conthawyin, Ottowatchkin, chiefs of the Ottawas and Chippewa nations of Indians, of the other part, do for ourselves and by the consent of the whole nation of Indians, witnesseth the said chiefs for and in consideration of five barrels of rum, three roles of tobacco, three pounds of vermillion and a belt of wampum, and three barrels of rum and three pounds of paint when possession was taken, valued 194 pounds 10 shillings, current money of the province of New York, to them in hand paid, the receipt whereof the said Indian chiefs doth hereby acknowledge, hath granted, bargained, sold, alienated and confirmed, and by these presents do hereby grant, bargain, sell, alien and confirm unto the said George MacDougall, his heirs and assigns forever the aforesaid island, that he may settle, cultivate or otherwise employ it to his majesty's advantage, as he shall think proper, the aforesaid island in the Detroit River, about three miles above the fort, together with all houses, out houses, appurtenances whatsoever on the said island, messuage or tenement and premises belonging or in any way appertaining, and also the reversion and reversions, remainder and remainders, rents and services of the said premises and every part thereof and all estate, right, title, claim and demand whatsoever, of them, the said Indians, of, in and to the said messuage and tenement and premises and every part thereof, to have and to hold the said messuage or tenement and all and singular the said premises above mentioned and every part and parcel thereof with the appurtenances unto the said George MacDougall, his heirs and assigns forever, and we, the above mentioned chiefs, do hereby engage ourselves, our heirs, our nations, executors, administrators and assigns forever to warrant and defend the property of the said island unto the said George MacDougall, his heirs, executors, administrators, and assigns forever against us or any person whatsoever claiming any right or title thereto."

This document was probably understood by the chiefs and those they represented to the extent of the consideration in rum and tobacco, but they traced their totems at the bottom. An effort to determine the species of the animals they undertook to draw forces the conclusion that they were inexperienced in the totem business or had been sampling the consideration.

Lord Hillsborough forwarded the memorial and deed to George III. and his council, but it probably got into a pigeonhole, for nothing more was heard of them. It is possible that George hinted to Lieut.-Gov. Hamilton that McDougall was to be given the dead state, for August 12, 1778, he wrote to Lieut.-Gov. Cramahe in relation to the Hog Island papers, and said:

"If Capt. McDougall should prosecute his pretensions in the courts, I want you to produce the claims of the inhabitants, which in my humble opinion are sufficient to support their title. An island being a royalty if it has ever been granted from the crown as a common, I apprehend the inhabitants have no power to surrender that right, as their posterity would thereby be injured past redress."

September 5, 1780, Maj. DePeyster, then the commandant at Detroit, had Nathan Williams and Jean Baptiste Crainte, able master carpenters, appraise the buildings McDougall had erected on the island, and then dispossessed him. The appraisers reported as follows:

One dwelling house	£250
One do do	40
One do do	10
An old barn without a top	18
A fowl house	6
Some timber	10
Total	£334

A month later De Peyster wrote to Gen. Haldimand that he had obeyed orders and placed loyalists upon Hog Island, and added: "The island is, however, sufficient for two substantial families only, there being much meadow ground and swamp on it, and being absolutely necessary to preserve

a run for the king's cattle, being the only place of security. I have sent your excellency a sketch of the island, which is only 768 acres. If I had placed more families there it would have augmented the expenses, and not have been cultivated so much to the advantage of the government."

McDougall's heirs, however, got possession again in 1784. Peace had been declared, and Lieut.-Gov. Hay saw a fine opportunity to be inexpensibly generous and magnanimously just. He was confident that when the boundary line was drawn Hog Island would be a portion of the United States, so he turned the disputed territory over to George and John Robert McDougall, sons of the old veteran lieutenant of his majesty's 24th.

November 11, 1793, the latter sold his undivided half of the island to William Macomb for 818 pounds and 16 shillings, and April 7 following Macomb bought the other half for 776 pounds. Macomb died in 1796, and bequeathed the island to his sons, John, William and David. When Detroit was evacuated by the British and the island came under the government of congress, all of the old claims, Indian, French and English, were ignored and the title confirmed to the Macombs. The shares of John and William passed to their brother, and March 3, 1817, David B. Macomb deeded the island to Barnabas Campau for $5,000. The remainder of the history of the Ile aux Cochons is uneventful and modern.

THE FIRST EDITOR HERE WAS FATHER GABRIEL RICHARD, THE PASTOR OF STE. ANNE'S.

FATHER GABRIEL RICHARD.
From a Cut in Possession of C. M. Burton.

Detroit's first editor was Father Gabriel Richard, the Catholic priest, the pastor of Ste. Anne's church.

After an interval of 60 years, Fr. Richard peers out of his picture grim and ancient, standing beside holy candles.

Thin and cadaverous, well he might be, for the life he led would have killed a horse.

The first newspaper printed in Detroit, or, indeed, west of the Alleghenies, dates back to the year 1809, the first page of which is here reproduced. It was only with great pains that the Journal was enabled to find a copy of this rare paper. It is known that there are only four copies of Father Richard's paper in existence, one of which is supposed to be in a museum or library at Worcester, Mass., while the other three are widely scattered. There is a copy in the hands of Mr. H. E. Baker and Mr. James H. Stone, the veteran editors, who own it jointly, and who long ago decided, when they are done with it, to deposit it in the Detroit Public Library. But in the meantime they value it as rubies. It is framed and kept under a glass, and the inflexible rule is to allow no copies or tracings to be made.

The "Essay" is a peculiar looking thing, for a newspaper, to modern eyes. It has the appearance of an opera house program or some such trifle as that. It is only four columns wide and is written in old-fashioned script type, the kind with the long "s," such as the modern reader is always mistaking for a letter "f."

The paper contains only one column of advertising, and that refers to books of the printing establishment, and was of course inserted without pay. The revenue was, then, to be derived from the subscription list solely. There is not a personal item in the paper, and scarcely a piece of news, in the modern acceptation of the term. There are a few paragraphs, clipped from other papers east, purporting to be news from the old world, but are just 67 days old.

There are a few scraps from New York, but they are not of great or exciting interest. The remainder of the paper consists of pious reflections and philosophic moralizings on such themes as "Happiness," "The Portrait of a True Friend," "Character," and such topics. The only item written for home use, apparently, is one which tells that the girls' school, of Ste. Anne's, is about to open, and parents are urged to send their girls to school. Some of the articles in the paper are written in French.

Father Richard was born October 15, 1764. His father was a gentleman of distinction, and his mother learned. He received ecclesiastical orders in 1790. He left France on account of the Revolution, and first settled in Baltimore. In due course he was called as a missionary, and visited the remote northwestern frontiers, until 1798, when he came to Detroit and founded the present church of Ste. Anne.

While on a visit to Boston, 1809, he bought a printing press and some type and published the first paper printed west of the Allegheny Mountains, the first number appearing August 31, 1809, called the "Michigan Essay, or Impartial Observer." The same year he published the first prayer book. Several numbers of the "Essay" were printed, but the population being scattered he thought best to suspend publication, there being no way to circulate the paper. All the printing was executed under his personal supervision.

The "Essay" was composed of four columns to a page 9½ by 10 inches in size. There are only four copies in existence. Some accounts say that Father Richard brought his press overland from Baltimore. Among the religious books printed were: La Journale du Chretien, 1811; Epistle and Gospel for Sundays and Holidays, 1812; a catechism. The press of Father Richard was subsequently used for printing deeds for the governor and judges of the territory, and when the English took possession they had Brock's proclamation printed on this press, it being the only establishment of this kind in the northwest.

The office of the "Essay" was removed after June 11, 1805, the day of the big Detroit fire, to Springwells, upon what was later a part of the Stanton farm. One part of the house was used to live in, another part was for the chapel, another for the printing office, and still another for the school.*

Father Richard's advocacy of American principles, 1812, and his denunciation of the British, excited great indignation in Canada, and he was soon afterwards seized and imprisoned at Sandwich, and was held captive until the close of the war, but during the interval was allowed to labor among the Indians. On his return to Michigan he found the people in great destitution, and went about collecting money and food in their behalf. In 1823 he was elected delegate to congress, being the first Roman Catholic priest to receive that honor. He won the esteem of the members, notably Henry Clay, who, when the abbe did not make his meaning clear, because of his defective use of English, frequently repeated his arguments to the house. He was defeated for re-election in 1826, and afterwards applied himself to works of piety and patriotism, built Indian schools at Green Bay, Arbre Croche, and St. Joseph's. He studied Sicard's method of teaching the deaf and dumb and delivered lectures. In 1832 he projected the foundation of a college. During the prevalence of the cholera Father

---

*The writer is in error. The printing press was not brought to Detroit until several years after the fire of 1805.—[C. M. B.

Richard was almost constantly on his feet day and night, until he was prostrated by disease, September 9, and died September 13, 1832.

Father Richard's introduction to the people is brief and to the point. He hopes to fulfil a long-felt want. He says:

THE ESSAY.

Detroit, August 31, 1809.

The Public are respectfully informed that THE ESSAY will be conducted in the utmost impartiality; that it will not espouse any political party; but fairly and candidly communicate whatever may be deemed worthy of insertion —whether Foreign, Domestic or Social.

* * * A noble aim be ours,
To mend the heart, to raise the pow'rs,
To show the world, on one extensive plan
All that is good and great and dear to man;
The patriot's plans and councils to display,
To point where glory shapes the warrior's way,
And as fresh wonders burst from every clime,
To mark the unfoldings of eventful Time,
That while our youth, with sparkling eyes shall read,
How heroes conquer, or more nobly bleed,
Their infant souls may catch the sacred flame
And join their country's love to that of Fame.

Gentlemen of talents are invited to contribute to our columns, whatever they suppose will be acceptable and beneficial—yet always remembering that nothing of a corrosive nature will be admitted.   THE PUBLISHER.

Father Richard had a "funny" department in his paper, under a big headline, thus:

HUMOROUS.

Count Tracey, complaining to Foote that a man had ruined his character, "So much the better," replied the wit, "it was a d—n bad one, and the sooner destroyed the better."

A mortal fever once prevailed upon a ship at sea; and a negro fellow was appointed to throw overboard the bodies of those who died, from time to time. One day, when the captain was on deck, he saw the negro dragging out of the forecastle the body of a sick man, who was struggling violently to free himself from the negro's grasp, and remonstrating against the cruelty of burying him alive. "What are you going to do with that man, you black d—l," said the captain, "don't you see that he moves and speaks?" "Why, yes, massa," replied the negro. "I know he say he no dead, but he always lie so like h—l, nobody nebber knows when to blieve him."

The "Essay" has its poet's corner, the word POETRY enscrolled in an attractive wreath of flowers. As usual, there is the big black headline, thus:

POETICAL.

(Written in the Country.)

The eve's in dusty mantle dres'd
The day's last gleam just streaks the west
Till slowly sinking from the hills
A deep'ning shade the prospect fills.

No sound to strike the ear doth move
From rural pipe or vocal grove,
The flocks and herds to rest are gone,
The hamlet's wonted sports are done.

The gathering clouds now close arrange
As waiting for the coming change
Till Luna and her train in sight
The sober evening yields to light.

OH HAPPINESS.

Oh, Happiness! where is thy resort?
Amidst the splendor of a court?
Or dost thou more delight to dwell
With humble hermit in his cell,
In search of truth? or doth thou rove
Thro Plato's academic grove?
Or else with Epicurus gay
Laugh at the farces mortals play?
Or with the graces doth thou lead
The sportive dance along the mead?
Or in Bellona's bloody car
Exult amid the scenes of war?
No more I'll search, no more I'll mind thee,
Fair Fugitive—I cannot find thee!

OMAR.

Among the miscellany, under bold headlines, is the following:

TRUE POLITENESS.

It is an evenness of soul, that excludes at the same time insensibility and too much earnestness—it supposes a quick discernment of the different characters, tempers, miseries, or perfections of mankind; and by a sweet condescension, adapts itself to each man's case. * * *

HAPPINESS—A FRAGMENT.

The scenes of my life have been sad, said a poor Frenchman, who had scrambled up one of the most precipitous mountains of North Wales and was now pensively leaning upon his stick and lending a mournful look toward a wide expanse of waters, which bounded his prospect. "The scenes of my life have been sad," silently repeated he, and a tear stole softly down his cheek, as the painful recollection of the past struck his soul—I have pursued the bubble, Happiness, all over the world, and have lived but to find it a delusion, a phantom of the brain. I have suffered the tortures of the inquisition, in Spain— I have been chained to the galleys in Italy—I have starved on the mountains of Switzerland— have languished beneath the Republican tyranny of France—and lastly, have been whipped as a vagabond, in England.

* * * Beneath the wide spreading branches, he constructed a simple hut; his meat was supplied by the roots and herbs of the valley; and the crystal spring, which

bubbled by his dwelling, afforded him a wholesome beverage. Every evening beheld him sinking blissfully to repose on his bed of leaves; and every dawning day saw him rise refreshed and cheerful. In a short time he discovered that he was happy. * * * After musing some time on the strangeness of the fact he found that the miseries of his past life were to be imputed to himself; that they arose from his own restlessness and ambition;—and that the true philosopher's stone, which converts everything it touches into gold, the real source of all human happiness is—contentment.

HUSBANDRY.

A receipt to keep cattle healthy by rubbing tar at the root of the horn.

A WANDERER'S COMPLAINT.

A brief article dealing with one who is equally restless everywhere.

EARLY RISING.

Anecdote telling how Buffon was pulled out of bed by his servant, Joseph, in order to learn the value of time.

MISCELLANEOUS.

A sentimental article called "The Portrait of a Real Friend."

MARKET REPORTS.

Rice, 7 dos 60 cts per cwt.
Logwood, $12.50 do.
Fustick, $9.60 do.
Coffee, 45@53 cts do.
Pimento, 43 cts do.
Pepper, 30 cts do.
Sugar, muscovado, 24@25 do.
Clayed, do 30@32 do.

Father Richard did not do a big advertising business, nor does he state the sworn paid circulation. His only "ads" are these:

At the Detroit Printing Office.

Pious Guide.
Perrin's French Grammar.
Book of Tales (66 engravings) 3 vols.
Columbian Orator.
Chambeau's French Grammar.
Wakefield's Family Tour Thro' Great Britain.
Way to Wealth, Dr. Franklin.

Youthful Recreations.
Youthful Sports.
Simple Stories.
English and French Catechisms.
Moral Fables.
Philadelphia Primer.
Footsteps in Natural History of Beasts.
Familiar Lessons.
Road to Learning.
Portraits of Curious Characters.
Jack of All Trades.
Father's Gift.
Letters From London.
True Piety.
Garden of the Soul.
Following Christ.
A Papist Misrepresented.
Geographical Cards.
Vade Mecum, Etc., Etc.

ACROSS THE RIVER.

(From the Detroit Journal, July 11, 1896.)

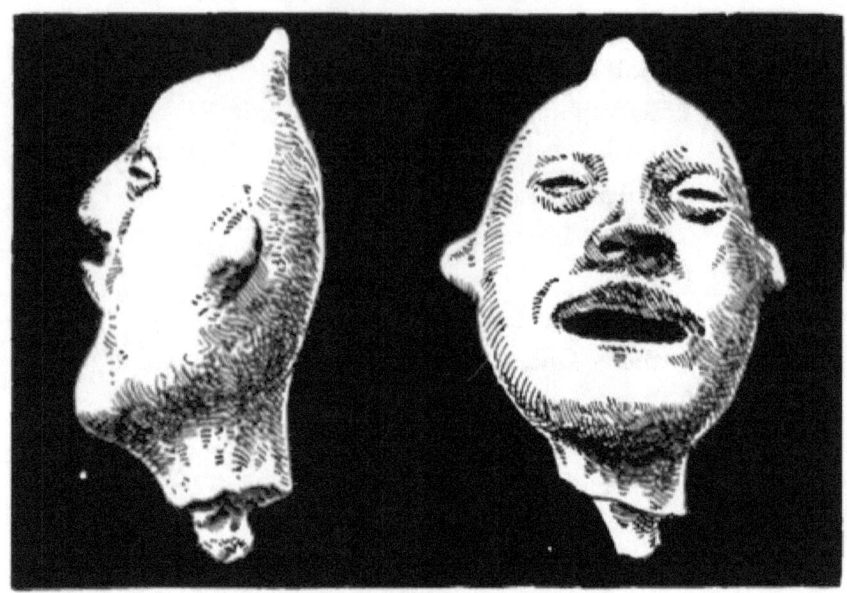

INDIAN STONE IMAGES.

Historic facts associated with the primitive town of Sandwich are fast fading into oblivion, because Canadian historians have failed to perpetuate them. Attentive only to strong strategic points as Quebec, Kingston and Little York, historians failed to give the only town of any importance in western Canada at the time the British evacuated Detroit any place on the pages of history. Instead of delving into musty documents for records of a century and a half ago they must be learned from the oldest residents whose grandmothers told them of the events.

The principal settlements along the Canadian frontier 100 years ago were from Sandwich westward to where the Detroit River empties into Lake Erie. Like nearly all Canada at that time, the French nationality predominated and the religion was Roman Catholic. That is why Canada did not join in the war for independence, because it preferred to be ruled by Protestant England, many thousand miles away, than by Protestant United States so near at hand. Without the discharge of a Canadian musket Canada got great good from the war of independence, because Great Britain, instead of ruling her with a hand of iron, as she was proceeding to do after the conquest of Canada, was forced to grant her many concessions to keep her from joining in the war for independence. Had Canadians been allowed the making of their own country, there would have been no Windsor, and Sandwich would have been the city of Western Canada; but Detroit's growth drew Canadians to the point opposite her. Windsor then grew into existence and grew when Detroit grew.

---

* In 1775 Sandwich was the trading post in western Canada for the Hudson Bay Company. When the peace negotiations which succeeded the Revolutionary war were completed and Michigan was ceded by the British to the United States, many persons who stubbornly maintained allegiance to King George moved across the river and settled along the frontier from Sandwich to Malden. It was then that Sandwich was made the seat of government for the western district, composed of Essex, Kent and Lambton counties. The town was a shipping point. All settlers were along

the river and used it as a waterway in the absence of passable roads. The settler's abode was a log hut or shanty, often built in a small clearing in the heart of the forest, and covered with bark or boughs. The nearest mill for grinding grain was 40 miles away, where Chatham now is. That there was little or no money was shown by the fact that a man would often carry a bushel of corn 40 miles to be ground, and then let the miller take his toll out of it instead of paying him; and so he had to carry the amount he gave in toll 40 miles for nothing.

The settler could make his own flour by pounding the grain in the hollow of a hardwood stump or grinding it in a little steel mill provided by the government. The few roads in existence in the swampy land were "corduroy roads," many of which can yet be found. Clothing was home spun and furniture home made, as also were carts and sleds.

"Logging bees" and "raisings" were held daily, and then distilled liquors were used in quantities. Once in a long time a preacher would visit the "sheep in the wilderness," and all the ceremonies required for a year would be done. Children would be baptized and marriages performed. There was no thought given to education when the settlers first located about Sandwich. The Jesuit fathers, principal among whom was Father La Salle, were the early spiritual advisers of the Catholics, and the Jesuits endured much privation to minister to the Indians. They settled at Sandwich nearly 200 years ago. All along the Detroit River they planted French pear trees. There were thousands of them, and they grew to be three feet in diameter and 70 feet high, but there are now less than a score of the trees. They were emblems of the gospel and the cross; were nursed by the tender care of the fathers in wet moss and intermingled with the primeval forest on both sides of the river. The Jesuits built a nunnery at Sandwich, which is still standing, although it was built before the evacuation of Detroit. Later, under the impression that Sandwich would be the city of Canada west, the splendid Catholic church and the celebrated L'Assumption college were built. The Hudson Bay Company's building was the largest in those parts, being five stories high. McIntosh had a trading post above Walkerville 100 years ago, and McGregors and Babys were conducting general stores at Sandwich. The Askin family were also traders and military men of note. The Patterson family were traders at Petite Cote, below Sandwich.

The dwelling around which cluster the most romantic associations is the Baby mansion on the river at Sandwich. Through its halls and corridors has sounded the voice of Gen. Brock, Gen. Proctor and of the forest heroes, Tecumseh and Splitlog. Gen. Hull made it his headquarters in 1812, and a year later was a prisoner there. Gen. Harrison, after the battle of the Thames, took possession of it and took Baby a prisoner. It was built over 100 years ago, and is now used as a boarding house.

St. John's Episcopal church was built at Sandwich at the time of the evacuation. Richard Pollard, who was sheriff and registrar, officiated as pastor. Pollard had been sheriff and registrar at Detroit, but he was a loyalist. When

Detroit was evacuated such records as were necessary to the new settler, and which were kept at the Detroit offices of the sheriff and registrar, were duplicated and transferred to the Sandwich office. The court of assize was held once a year at Sandwich for the three counties, a territory of 2,817 square miles.

While the settlers on the Canadian side were French mainly, the business men were Scotch. A century ago there were 20,000 inhabitants in Canada, and in other parts of Canada the English and Scotch were the traders. Few of them were successful, because they had been accustomed to the comforts of the old land, and knew little about the ways of the new country. The U. E. Loyalists, when they crossed the border, were given grants of 200 acres each, and, being thrifty and used to privations, prospered. It was not until there were 2,200 people in Detroit that Windsor became a settlement. Then she began to draw from Sandwich and the west, and the firms of Cameron & McDonald, James Dougall, Blackadder & Brown, James Lambie, and the late John Curry, formed the business portion of the town.

The only ferries then were two log canoes, run by Pierre St. Amour, who kept a hotel where Ouellette avenue and Sandwich street now are, and by Francis Labalaine. The price for the round trip was four times the cost that it is by ferry steamer now.

The Ottawa Indians, whose chief was Pontiac, inhabited the Canadian side much of the time. Pontiac had slept in the Baby mansion as a guest. Their spear heads and arrow points of flint are often found along the river bank. G. R.

M. Pentland, of Peters street, Sandwich, has hundreds of Indian relics. One of these is the head of a god whose mouth is open and eyes partly closed, in the act of blessing the Indians, and who was worshiped by the Indians then inhabiting Essex county.

The first execution at Sandwich was over 100 years ago. A white man and a negro were gibbeted on the highway for murdering a girl in Kent county.

THE FORT IN 1792.

(From the Detroit Journal, July 11, 1896.)

There is no report upon the condition of the fortress at the time it became United States property, but it must have been in a sorry plight, and well nigh useless for defensive purposes. Possibly this is the reason why the residents said nothing about the acquisition in their letters.

The last report upon its condition to be found in the Canadian archives is in series B, volume 60, page 228. It was made by Benjamin Fisher, Capt. Commanding, Royal Engineers, in the fall of 1792, and is as follows:

"Detroit: The principal services now executing at this place consist in such repairs as are more immediately necessary to the officers' and soldiers' barracks; erecting a flagstaff, removing 12 platforms, and repairing 5 others in Fort Lernoult.

"With respect to such further services as may be necessary for the year 1793, it is not an easy matter for me to determine without knowing to what extent government may choose to go in re-establishing the post, or the importance in which it is viewed.

"The decayed state of the buildings, and the insecurity of the defenses of the town from the ruinous condition of the blockhouses and picketing, has been already reported on by board of survey, and since more fully by Lieut. Pilkinton of the Royal Engineers. I shall therefore state generally the condition of the works and buildings in the fort, citadel, town and naval yard, accompanying the report with separate estimates, and submitting to better judgment the propriety of incurring so heavy an expense as appears requisite to reinstate the works and buildings of the post.

"Fort Lernoult—The greater part of the interior slope of the ramparts requires fresh sodding, the magazine to be repaired, and the position of the entrance changed. The sheds for the fixed ammunition are bad, and from their proximity to other buildings and to the magazine, endanger the safety of the place in case of fire. A new one is, therefore, proposed. New drip-board and several new waterspouts are wanting to the barracks. The sallyport is quite rotten, unsafe, and injurious to the health of men occasionally confined there; the main drain very offensive; the fraize and picketing in the ditch much decayed; the ditch requires in many parts to be cleaned, and the counterscarp repaired. The grate, bridge and abattis are good. The magazine contiguous to the fort wants some trifling repairs for its security, for it is to be apprehended from the whole tenor of the building that it will not be of long duration.

"Citadel: The barracks in general require plastering, whitewashing and repairs to the hearths and chimneys; 32 new sashes are wanted, as also two additional ones for the hospital to give a freer communication of air. The barrack stores are mostly placed in the upper story of the men's barracks, as are also the artillery stores. The latter, from their great weight, not only render such a disposition very inconvenient, but endanger great the building, which is slight. The picketing of the citadel and woodyard is wholly decayed.

"Town: The picketing on the water side is good, but from Fort Lernoult to the water on the east side is quite rotten, and in many places supported by props. The same on the west side, excepting the salient parts contiguous to the blockhouses. The blockhouses Nos. 1 and 2 are wholly decayed, and unsafe even to the removal of the cannon now in them. The water blockhouse is secure for the present, but not worthy of considerable repairs. West blockhouse may last some time with common repairs, but the one in the barrack yard, which at present serves as commissary and barrack master's stores, is quite decayed. These blockhouses are at present raised on upright frames 12 feet high. If they are to be reinstated I should recommend an alteration in the construction, and that their lower frame might be converted into a storeroom or useful apartment, which would add but little to the expense. The east platform by the river is on too slight a frame to be secure, and the west platform is wholly rotten. This latter is commanded by a bank, which is an accumulation of rubbish from the town, and should be removed. The

Indian store is so wholly decayed that any repairs would be injudicious. A frame building, 60 feet by 30, is recommended for the accommodation of Indian artillery and storekeeper general's stores. It may be eligibly placed in the citadel behind the barracks. The weighty stores being in the lower part, frame work will be sufficient. The artillery carriages require painting. Twenty traveling magazines are wanting. Ladders and sentry boxes much wanted.

"Naval yard: Is surrounded only by a slight picketing, and without the protection of the garrison. The naval storehouse is so completely decayed that props are fixed on all sides to prevent its falling. The building at present consists of two stories, and is 85 feet by 22. The lower story is the store, and the upper one a working place for riggers. Both places are sufficiently large for the purpose to which they are applied, but as a fire in winter is necessary for the riggers, I thought it advisable to have a detached building for them, and have estimated accordingly. This building is, I apprehend, so essentially necessary for the fitting out and repair of the vessels on the lakes that it is necessary it should be early attended to. If it is judged expedient to reconstruct the naval storehouse in the way proposed, I should recommend a deviation in the line of picketing, advancing at the same time the blockhouse No. 2, for should it not inclose a more eligible spot for a dockyard than at present occupied, it at least offers a secure and convenient situation for the naval buildings.

"I have offered little more than is necessary for the re-establishing the works and buildings of the post. How far the present circumstances and situation of it render such a measure advisable is not for me to determine."

THE OLD LANDMARKS.
(From the Detroit Journal, July 11, 1896.)

A retrospect of Detroit for the last hundred years properly includes recollections of the township of Springwells, the greater portion of which, territorially, has been absorbed into the city.

DETROIT IN 1838.
From an Engraving Owned by C. M. Burton.

Fifty years ago the western limits of Detroit were a little beyond Seventh street. The only highways open in that direction were the River road, the Chicago road, now called Michigan avenue, and the Grand River road. The chief thoroughfare was the River road, for the country back of that was principally forest. The heavy growth of timber, the clay soil, which held the accumulated rains and snows and the insufficient drainage retarded settlement. The flood of eastern people who came in the late '30s and the early '40s to make homes for themselves in Michigan, did not remain in Detroit, but made for the southern and central tiers of counties, where the land was easier cleared and the agricultural resources of the most magnificent promise. Between Detroit and Dearborn there were few improved farms, except upon the river front and along the borders of the Rouge. The old French preference for living near a water course was manifested by the newer immigrants if by that term we can designate the enlightened, adventurous and energetic sons and daughters of New England and New York who hurried to Michigan to lay the foundation of the young state. They made homes for themselves on the borders of the Rouge, the Ecorse, Raisin, Clinton, Huron, Grand, St. Joseph, Shiawassee, Huron, St. Clair and Saginaw Rivers.

Fifty years ago the depot of the Michigan Central had freshly been removed from the Michigan avenue site of the city hall to its present location on the river at the foot of Third street. At this point emptied the River Savoyard, which had its source in a rivulet near where St. Mary's Catholic church now stands, at St. Antoine st. and Monroe avenue. It meandered down toward Cadillac square, and the site of the new county buildings, where it broadened out into a lagoon. Water fowl and water snakes, the impetuous blue-racer among them, found a congenial habitat there. The Savoyard deepened and its current became more forceful as it approached the line of Woodward avenue. It is on record in Farmer's History that batteaux freighted with stone for old Ste. Anne's church, navigated to the corner of Bates and Congress, the present armory of the Light Infantry being erected on the grounds once confined within the church plot. We know that there was a bridge across the Savoyard at Griswold street, and that Levi E. Dolsen, an old citizen, well known in his generation, who died a year or two ago, fell from the bridge while fishing and was nearly drowned.

In excavating a few years ago the foundation for Phelps, Brace & Co.'s and Lee & Cady's buildings, cannon balls and other military relics were unearthed. They were souvenirs of the British occupation, and the cannon balls may have been aimed at Pontiac's red horde of savages.

The waters of the Savoyard began to be intercepted and led off by sewers 50 years ago, the stream dwindled and was filled up, and when the new Michigan Central station was constructed its last vestiges disappeared. Last fall, in constructing a building opposite the Wayne Hotel on River street, the hull of a small craft was unearthed, which no doubt was left to decay in the shallow Savoyard.

A walk down the River road in those days would have taken the pedestrian along a tolerably high bank which faced the street from Fifth street to Eighth. This walk was guarded by a hand rail. From its elevation one could see the new city gas works, then just put in operation. The ruined old building now belongs to Frederick Stearns and is used as a marble and stone shop. The young firm of Jackson & Wiley had a foundry nearly opposite that was worked to its limit night and day. The railroad company had a peculiar machine which turned out from billets of wood oblong oval wedges that were used to make firm the joints of the T rails, then newly used—the antecedent of the fish plate. There was a car shop of considerable dimensions along the side of the street, and by an hydraulic machine, attended by Bijah Joy, of subsequent fame as a policeman who passed "an hour at the central station" every day. By means of this machine car wheels were forced upon their axles. Next was the railroad machine and blacksmith shop, and round house, made significant by what was said to be the tallest chimney in America, only exceeded in height by the St. Rollux chimney at Glasgow, Scotland. This chimney and busy shops, for which it once produced the desired air drafts, were long ago demolished.

The railroad track struck the river at the mouth of May's Creek, between Eleventh and Twelfth streets, but before coming to it one passed the farms of John Mullett, the old-time surveyor, and Gov. Woodbridge. Mullett and Woodbridge lived in old-style French mansions. A part of the Mullett residence still stands back of the Hammond Beef Company's warehouse. Next was that of John S.

Abbott and Henry T. Backus, sons-in-law of Gov. Woodbridge. Magnificent French pear trees were the surroundings of each of these dwellings, and of every other dwelling on the river front.

The railroad track, when it reached the river, was carried by trestle work over the shallows up to the channel bank, and thence in a straight line to Third street. There was at first but a single track, and the trains as they passed over it reverberated loudly. The water inclosure formed by the trestle reached from Fifth to Eleventh street. The early formations of ice were protected by the closely driven piles and thereby made the space into a skating park that was much besought by the youth of the city.

A bridge carried the road over May's Creek, just west of Woodbridge's mansion. The rest of the way, except from Fourteenth street to Twenty-fourth, the highway followed the margin of the river. The first reach of the river was a sort of rendezvous for scows and small sail craft. There was a couple of taverns of some note—one kept by Thomas Lyon, an eccentric Englishman, formerly a soldier, whose wife, a buxom lady, was a typical old-time landlady. The other was kept by Louis Specht, a German from the region of the upper Rhine, whose knowledge of the French language made him congenial to the sailors and farmers below. Saw mills were just erected in this district, one by Selah Reeve, the other by Bela Hubbard, and John F. King. There were tanneries also, one of them superintended by the Levi F. Dolsen named above.

Another small stream crossed the highway just below the Godfrey mansion. Vestiges of this stream are apparent today south of Fort street in front of Peter Henkel's house.

The River road then kept inland. It passed the home of William Burtchell—generally called Billy—a noted steamboat runner. On the front of the Loranger farm, now known as the Lafontaine farm, was an extensive fishery, perhaps the best on the river. Old Jean Baptiste Loranger had a merry crew of French fishermen, who sang as they rowed out to cast their nets, and gave exultant Gallic shouts when the catch warranted such enthusiasm. They lived in shanties on the river's edge. Fish, potatoes, bread, pork and beans were the staple articles on the bill of fare, and the hungry stranger was always invited to sit with them at the feast. Whiskey was 15 cents a gallon, and probably the dampness of their occupation caused them to take more of it than was good for them.

Continuing on, the wayfarer came to the residence of Maj. Henry Brevoort, a veteran of Perry's victory and other campaigns of 1812. Maj. Brevoort had a French pony and a low hung buggy, covenient for a man of his stature and portliness. Every day he would drive up to the city to call upon friends. It was a tradition of the neighborhood that he received a silver dollar—"the dollar of the daddies"—every time he went to town, in the way of payment on his pension. This, of course, is not the way pensions are paid, but the story was told that he collected his dollar every day.

Passing beyond Brevoort's, the River road ran to the edge of a high, steep bank, exactly like the bank to be seen today on the Windsor side of the river. It started from about where the Detroit Gas Works are now located and continued past Twenty-fourth street. There was a sort of bay here, the water being so shallow that boys seeking

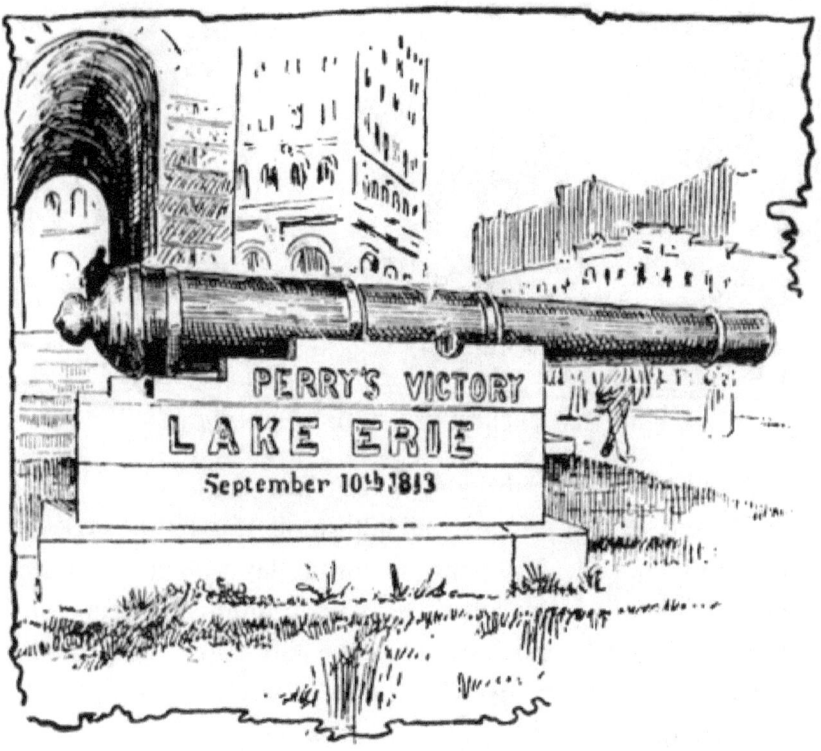

the place to bathe could wade out 200 feet before getting beyond their depth. Some vestiges of the bank remain. The old brick mansion of Gov. Porter, occupied in recent times by the late Sylvester Larned, stood uninhabited on this high bank, commanding a grand view of the river. Another bit of neighborhood gossip, told in whispers by the French lads who lived thereabout—C. Peter Lafferty and Samuel Campau will remember about it—was a story that the house was haunted.

AN OLD FRENCH HOUSE ON THE ROUGE.

The road was graded down from the bank to the river level, and at the foot of the hill stood the Eagle tavern, celebrated as the headquarters for a day and a night of Gen. William Henry Harrison, who brought his army up this way to take possession of the city after the British forces, subsequent to 1812 and Perry's victory, had vacated it.

Continuing on, the fishing grounds of James Harper, who had married the widow of Jean Baptiste Campau, was a conspicuous feature, especially during the whitefish season. Knaggs' Creek, lined with cattails, bullrushes, water lilies, and muskrat houses, emptied into the river just below. Some years later Lewis Ives dammed up the stream, excavated its channel, built a pier and converted the bed of

Knaggs' Creek into a drydock, the first on the great lakes The remains of Ives' dock are still to be seen.

Here stood for many years the last of the old windmills on the river bank. Farmer's History gives a picture of it.

THE WINDMILL IN 1838.

Lower down, about where Edward Campau used to live, or rather on the site of Clark's drydock, was another fishery. The road then passed in front of the finest dwelling houses on the river, then the property of Gen. John E. Schwartz, who had much to do with the militia, and whose official uniform was the most gorgeous worn in all this region.

When the government bought the front of the Forsyth farm and began to build Fort Wayne, the road was deflected from the river front through the farms to the rear, cutting across the Williams and the Reeder farms, in the line which is followed today. The old Williams farm houses were converted into a tavern by the late eccentric 'Squire Samuel Ludlow. He called the place Buena Vista hall, in honor of Gen. Taylor, and the Whigs of that day put up a great pole with a Taylor and Fillmore flag. Zach Chandler was one of the leading spirits. The Democrats, not to be outdone, put up a pole for Gen. Cass at Abiel Wood's place on the Reeder farm, and Robert Henderson displayed a large oil painting of Cass in his treaty with the Menominee Indians at Green Bay. This picture would be valuable—in a historical sense—for the Detroit public library, as it contained many portraits of old-time Michigan notables. What has become of it it is hard to say. Some of the French people, Eli Barkume, Clement Lafferty or others who knew Bob Henderson, can perhaps put inquirers on the track of it.

Edwin Reeder, a man of great learning and some peculiarities, inclined to conviviality, lived upon his farm, the front of which consisted of high banks of sand, comparing in elevation to the counterscarp of Fort Wayne. Out of this sand bank exuded many springs of pure water. From the abundance of these springs the name Springwells was derived. Reeder himself, although an Englishman, had a romantic fancy for the early French settlers, and was always hopeful of having the name Springwells changed to Bellefontaine. He never succeeded in doing so.

The Reeder sand banks have all been leveled, and the sand hauled away to make foundations for street pavements in the city. In removing the sand the skeletons of Indians buried there, and of soldiers of Harrison's army, and those of the Americans who campaigned here in 1812, were found. The late John Greusel established one of the first brick yards on the river in front of the Reeder farm. Previous to that the brick used in the city came from yards up the River Rouge.

Passing along the rear of Fort Wayne, the River road skirted an extensive marsh, then known as Prairie Ronde. The Wabash railroad track now goes through the center of it, and the marsh has become the site of the rich truck gardens that front on Fort street. Leaving the marsh, it passed close to a long Indian mound, a burial place where the skeletons of mound builders have been exhumed. The skeletons have been described in articles written by Bela Hubbard and Prof. Henry Gilman; the Smithsonian Institution has published accounts of them. There was little of cultivated ground here until one reached the point where the River road struck the Rouge, conspicuous by a high bluff of sand, which overlooks the great marsh, of late years given over to the improving hand of business, prompted by the sagacity of Henry B. Ledyard, Henry Russel and their associates. On this sand hill stood a solitary tavern, kept by the Widow McGregor, then called the Junction house. Beyond this the French held sway all the way to Ecorse. French ponies in great herds wandered freely all about the territory. The owners corralled them once a year and branded them with their initials. Very hardy little beasts, pawing away the snow in winter to get at the sweet, dry grass below, and sometimes making trouble to the new clearings which the settlers had established. Some of these French ponies had speed, particularly the pacers. One could see them in all their glory, likewise their owners, in their manifestations of voluble excitement, at the racing on the ice on the long, straight stretch of the Rouge that extends past the present glass works. They raced their ponies, they hunted mink and muskrats, they gathered the French pears and cherries, they cultivated their little farms, and lived happy and placid lives, not much disturbed by modern innovations.

DETROIT IN 1857.
From an Engraving Owned by C. M. Burton.

It was a time of peace and plenty, and about as much of happiness as satisfies a simple-minded community, and that perhaps expresses all the contentment of life, which of itself is the definition of happiness.

ONE HUNDRED YEARS AGO.

(From the Detroit Journal, July 11, 1896.)

The Stars and Stripes have waved over this city 100 years. It is now nearly 200 years since the founding of Detroit. It is two years older than St. Petersburg. Nearly one-half of this time was under British and French rule. The history of the first half is not very extensive, and of but little importance, except as it had bearing on the latter half. The hundredth anniversary of the hauling down of British colors is being celebrated in Detroit today with imposing and impressive ceremonies. It is a date that should be remembered, in this busy day, apt to be forgotten, and the events form a patriotic lesson that is good and wholesome.

It is remarkable that a comprehensive account of this event, the most momentous in the history of the great northwest, has never been written, or, if written, has not been preserved. The territory that by the evacuation of Detroit, and the military posts to the north and south passed from British to American rule, was greater in area than the 13 states that had won independence 13 years before after a struggle unparalleled in the history of the oppressed in all nations, and yet this event is chronicled in our school histories, if mentioned at all, as having occurred in 1796, a single line telling a tale of more moment to the millions of America than the surrender of Cornwallis.

Early histories of Detroit have no more than a mention of the fact, but probably for the reason that no more was known. The date, even, was uncertain until a few years ago, when a local historian settled the question by finding official correspondence of Col. Hamtramck that was carried away when Hull surrendered the city to the British in 1812.

C. M. Burton has at great expense collected together a mass of information concerning Detroit and Michigan from the days of Cadillac to the present time. He has found it in old bookstores in this country, Canada and England; in libraries, and the treasured archives of nations; but wherever and whenever found he has become the owner if possible, and if not, has procured manuscript copies. All these books, pamphlets, records, manuscripts, and letters he placed at the disposal of the Journal when it asked the privilege of compiling a comprehensive report of the events of July 11, 1796, and those immediately preceding and following them.

To get one fact here, another there; one from a letter written within the palisades to a friend at a distance; another from a military order, or a moldy book of travels, in which "f's" are used for "s's," and bring them together chronologically, required time and patience, but the Journal gave both to the work. How well, or how indifferently, that work has been done, the public can determine from the supplement to this edition.

It is the first compilation that has ever been attempted, but it is unsatisfactory, because the data are not to be obtained. It is possible that the journal of Gen. Wayne

FORT LERNOULT AT THE END OF THE REVOLUTION.

contained a graphic description of how the crestfallen British marched out with trailing arms and silent drum, and how the Americans triumphantly entered the fortress to the music of "Yankee Doodle"; how the soldiers cheered and the eagle screamed when the Stars and Stripes rose proudly to the top of the flagstaff at high noon of that day, but, unfortunately for the writer of evacuation day history 100 years after, the volumes of "Mad Anthony's" reports for 1796 have disappeared from the national library and cannot be found.

A LEGEND OF 1796.

(From the Detroit Journal, July 11, 1896.)

One of Maj. Gladwin's soldiers at Fort Pontchartrain, Detroit, a little over 100 years ago, was Sergt. Jimmie Campbell. He had said a lover's adieu to Mary Macdonald when he left Boston to join his regiment at Detroit. For many months after leaving Boston he heard from her often. She ceased to write, and Jimmie heard no more of her until finally he learned that she was to be married to Capt. Charles Stewart, who had been Jimmie's rival, and whom Mary had once rejected. The thought of this made Jimmie reckless. His yearning for a perilous exploit was gratified a few hours later. A vessel with reinforcements and provisions was en route from Fort Erie to Fort Pontchartrain. Maj. Gladwin feared that it would be surprised and plundered by the allied tribes of the Hurons, Wyandottes and Pottawattomies. He then learned through J. D. Baby, a trader, whose agent, Laflamboise, had located the tribes, that his fears had been well grounded. Sergt. Campbell knew that Maj. Gladwin wanted a warning given to the captain of the vessel. He was an expert with a canoe, and when he volunteered to do the hazardous task Gladwin accepted. The young sergeant started for Riviere au Canard. He affected the guise of a trader. He found the Hurons, Wyandottes and Pottawattomies camped on the two banks of Riviere au Canard. The warriors were making bows and arrows of the young hickory. The squaws were twisting deer skin and the inner bark of elm for bow strings, and tying wild turkey feathers on the arrows, and the poisoned flint barb was being inserted in slit and tied with the finest thread of the raccoon gut. Meeting the daughter of a Huron chief, Campbell gave her many strings of beads, gaudy cloth and bracelets.

"You braves are very busy. Why is it?"

"When the vessel of the pale face reaches Turkey Island, braves take her."

Campbell hastened down the river to the vessel, which was making such slow progress in a calm that he decided to return in advance of her and watch the Indians. Campbell had been watched by Indian scouts, and when he returned to Canada he was captured, and after the attack was made and disastrously repulsed he was sentenced to death as a spy. A rescuing party found him afterwards with an arm and leg mutilated so that they had to be amputated, and his face was shockingly disfigured, but he was alive.

He was taken to Fort Pontchartrain. A message awaited him. It was from Mary, and said that she had left Boston for Detroit. She explained her long silence by saying that she had been thrown from her horse, her brain being affected by the injury; fever had set in, and then followed one of those remarkable cases that physicians know instances of where a patient's memory has become blank to a certain date, and memory distinctly recalls everything prior to that date. So Mary claimed she had forgotten Jimmie, remembered only her first sweetheart, Capt. Stewart, and became engaged to marry him. It was upon her wedding morn, she claimed, that her memory returned, and she was now coming to see Jimmie.

Jimmie read the note again and again.

"Too late, too late!" he said, with childlike sobs.

Next day the door of Jimmie's room was gently opened and a beautiful girl entered. It was Mary. The sunlight shed its lustre around her, and it shone upon Jimmie. Mary had been told nothing of her sweetheart's condition. As she looked upon his disfigured face, once so handsome, and his mutilated limbs, she became dazed, startled, and with a feeling of horror she uttered a cry of anguish and rushed from the room.

The regimental physician found the laudanum bottle empty beside Jimmie's bed, and they buried him with martial honors.

CAUSE OF THE DELAY.

(From the Detroit Journal, July 11, 1896.)

As stated in another article, the independence that was won for the east by the success of the armies of the colonies in 1783 was not extended to the northwest territory until 1796, when the Jay treaty went into effect and the boundary line was established.

Prof. A. C. McLaughlin, in a paper read before the American Historical Association in 1894, on "The Western Posts and the British Debts," gives the reasons why England retained possession of this territory for 13 years after the close of the Revolution.

A preliminary treaty of peace was agreed upon by representatives of Great Britain and the United States at Paris, November 30, 1782, but a definite treaty was not signed until September 3, 1783, and was not ratified by congress until January 14 following, or by Great Britain until April 9. This instrument provided that Great Britain should, "with all convenient speed," withdraw all her armies, garrisons and fleets from the United States, and from every post, place and harbor within the same."

Hostilities had ceased, under an armistice, January 20, 1783, and Gen. Carleton was ordered to vacate New York as early as April, but it was November before the last of his troops were withdrawn. In July of that year Gen. Washington sent Gen. Steuben to Quebec to request a transfer of the posts in the northwest. Gov. Haldimand refused to consider the matter of evacuation, on the ground that he had received no orders on the subject. In March of the next year Gov. Clinton, of New York, sent Col. Fish to Gov. Haldimand with a request that he be notified when his majesty intended to evacuate the posts within that state. Haldimand replied that the treaty being with congress, it would be inadmissible to grant the posts to a single state.

In June, Gen. Knox, made a formal demand in the name of the United States, but without result. It was claimed by Haldimand that the United States had not complied with the treaty; that the Indians and royalists were opposed to a change of masters, and that the fur trade at Detroit and other points would suffer from a change. It was also claimed that the loyalists were persecuted by the Americans and their estates confiscated.

In August, 1785, John Adams, the American minister, was told by Pitt at London, that the delay in evacuating the posts was due to impediments interposed by the American states to the recovery of debts due to British creditors, to which Adams replied that nothing of the kind was stipulated in the treaty; that no government ever undertook to pay the private debts of its subjects. Prof. McLaughlin says:

"Doubtless the Americans had broken the treaty. The treatment of the loyalists forms no bright chapter in our national history. Several states had laws on their statute books which prevented the ready recovery of debts by British creditors. The war left the country in a condition of financial demoralization. It is not surprising that the foreign merchant, who seemed in some of the states to hold a permanent lien on property and to be a lasting drag on progress, should find statutes and stay-laws blocking his path. In October, 1786, Jay made a report to congress in which he found many of the charges true. In November he wrote to Adams as the result of his inquiries into the conduct of the states that there had not been a single day since it took effect on which it has not been violated by one or other of the states."

Jay further declared that "deviation on our part preceded any on the part of Great Britain," and added that England was not under obligations to evacuate our territory until after the ratification of the treaty of peace, and the acts of some of the states he considered the first violation of the treaty.

In 1787, upon the suggestion of Jay, congress passed an act recommending to the several states that all laws repugnant to the treaty of peace be repealed. This was done by all the states, though Virginia made her repealing act conditional upon England giving up the posts.

When Washington became president he requested Gov. Morris, who was in London, to represent to the British ministry that the new federal court had been given full jurisdiction over cases arising under the treaty, and to ask the ministry what objections remained to fulfilling its terms. As a result of this interview England sent a minister to this country, and he and Jefferson entered upon a consideration of the differences to a substantial ratification of the treaty. Hammond demanded that all debts be paid, and confiscated estates of tories restored. Congress had recommended that this be done, and Jefferson contended that this action constituted a fulfillment of the treaty, because recommendation was all our commissioners promised.

When Jay went to England in 1794, England was at war with France, and did not deem it best to provoke an alliance of the United States with that country. The Indians were continually committing depredations, and the Americans charged that they were incited to hostilities by the British within our borders. The Americans were ripe for war, and Jay found the British ministry ready and willing to agree upon terms of permanent peace. The treaty then negotiated provided for the evacuation of all frontier posts on or before June 1, 1796, and for a commission to determine the amount of debt due British merchants, which, in case collection had been hindered by lawful impediments, was to be assumed by our government.

LA MOTHE CADILLAC.

HOW HE CAME TO FOUND A SETTLEMENT HERE.

(From the Detroit Journal, July 11, 1896.)

How long there had existed an encampment at the spot on which Detroit now stands, there is now no way to determine. Certain it is that when Cadillac came in 1701 he was met by a handful of *coureurs-de-bois*, who were living here and trading with the savages.

It is to Antoine de la Mothe Cadillac that we owe the founding of this beautiful city of ours, though someone sooner or later, in the general colonization of the new world, must have perceived the advantages, both military and commercial, of the site.

Lamothe Cadillac, as he signed himself, was born in a little hamlet in the southeastern part of France. Other than the date of his birth, March 5, 1658, and his baptism five days later, we have no authentic facts concerning his life, until we find him in the new world, a lieutenant in the king's service, marrying beautiful Theresa Guyon, the daughter of a Quebec merchant. After distinguishing himself by energetic service in Acadia, he received from Frontenac command of the fort and Indian mission at Mackinac. Here it is he conceived the idea which is of such direct interest to us. Imbued with the idea that a settlement somewhere on the banks of the strait, now called Detroit River, would be of the greatest military value, and that in time it might be successful as a colony, he secured his release from the position at Mackinac and set sail for France to present in person to the king his arguments in favor of establishing the post. His plans meeting with approval, the colonial minister, Count Pontchartrain, gave him the necessary authority and allowed him the equivalent of $275 for building the fort.

He returned to America in the spring of 1701 and went directly to Montreal. After some weeks of preparation he set out with 100 soldiers and Canadians, and 25 canoes, carrying, besides the men, all that was necessary for the construction of the fort and village. De Tonty was second in command. Leaving Montreal, the expedition entered the Ottawa River. By ascending this, which gave them a path almost directly west, and crossing by land to Georgian Bay, they reached Lake Huron.

Finally, after toiling over six weeks against current and through forest, on one beautiful morning in July they glided with the current down the giant river; and, coming out from behind the luxuriously wooded Belle Isle, beheld their future home. And as he saw spread before him a low hill about 700 yards from the river, stretching along for over two miles, and dotted with beautiful groves, what visions of a great city, with a stately avenue on that ridge, must have passed before the eyes of Cadillac. Landing at a small cove which lay where the foot of Griswold street does now, the leader staked off the sites of the palisade and magazine, and by sundown Frere Constantin summoned the garrison of Fort Pontchartrain to their first vespers.

Surrounded on all sides by 200 miles of semi-hostile Indians, with no approach except by water, Detroit's growth was necessarily slow. The tide of settlement had not reached it. Under 13 different commandants for the French king, the number of homes increased very slowly, in spite of repeated offers on the part of the Canadian government to furnish each settler with farming utensils and to support his family for the first year. For we know that even in 1805 the number of houses in Fort Pontchartrain, as it was still called, was something less than 200, and the greater part of these were within the stockade, clustered about the little street called Ste. Anne, which, though only 30 feet wide, lay in almost the same position as Jefferson avenue does now. There was one house of two stories near the center of the stockade.

Up to 1760 the French had succeeded in little more than keeping possession of the position. Now in the French and Indian war at the surrender of Montreal, and with it the whole northwest territory, our city passed into the hands of the English. The condition of the inhabitants underwent no change at all, as a fact, except that occasioned by their taking the oath of allegiance to Great Britain, and the removal of the French troops.

But at this change to control by the arrogant English, the Indians, who had with such difficulty been kept in peace by the conciliatory policy of the French, aroused by the burning eloquence of Pontiac, hatched a scheme for getting possession of all the land held by the English. Detroit, in Pontiac's well laid plan, was to be taken by treachery. In the simultaneous attack on all the forts from Mackinac to the east, Detroit, with one other station, held out. How the plan failed because of the forewarning given by Catherine, the Ojibway girl, we all know by heart. Now commenced the six months' siege, during which the defeat of a part of the garrison at Bloody Run happened, and our beautiful pleasure ground, Belle Isle, was converted into a slaughter yard by the massacre of a detachment who were captured while coming as a reinforcement for the worn-out garrison. Finally, after the news of the treaty of peace between France and England, the Indians lost heart and slowly drew off.

A few years after this, during the American Revolution, Maj. Lernoult, who was stationed here with 500 men, erected a large earth fort on the ground which is now covered by four squares directly in the rear of our city hall. This fort was called Lernoult until during the war of 1812, when it was changed to Shelby in honor of the hero of the Battle of the Thames. About this time, instead of "The Village on the Strait," the city began to be styled simply Detroit.

In 1783, by the treaty acknowledging the independence of the states, Detroit was claimed by the new government. This was disputed by the Canadian authorities, and in the other difficulties which the new republic was undergoing no resistance was made to the British, who obstinately remained in the fort until 1796, when the boundary on the whole northwest territory, including Detroit on the American side, was definitely placed by the Jay treaty. On the 11th day of July, 1796, the British troops withdrew from Detroit.

A few days later, when Capt. Porter, with a detachment of Wayne's army, took possession, they found the wells choked up with stones and all the windows in the barracks broken by the British soldiery in a feeling of chagrin and defeat.

www.ingramcontent.com/pod-product-compliance
Lightning Source LLC
Chambersburg PA
CBHW021732220426
43662CB00008B/813